THAT RIBBON OF HIGHWAY I:

Highway 99 From the Oregon Border to the State Capital

By Jill Livingston

Photographs By Kathryn Golden Maloof

ISBN 0-9651377-3-2

First printing 1996, Second printing 1998
Second edition, First Printing 2000, Second Printing 2005

Cover photo of Dog Creek Bridge and all contemporary photos and drawings by Kathryn Golden. Maps by Jill Livingston. Book design by Living Gold Press. Title from *This Land is Your Land* by Woody Guthrie.

Library of Congress Cataloging-in-Publication Data
Livingston, Jill.
That ribbon of highway I : Highway 99 from the Oregon border to
the state capital / by Jill Livingston ; photographs by Kathryn
Golden Maloof.— 2nd ed.
p. cm.
Includes bibliographical references (p.) and index.
ISBN 0-9651377-3-2 (pbk. : alk. paper)
1. California, Northern—Guidebooks. 2. United States Highway
99—Guidebooks. 3. United States Highway 99—History. 4.
California, Northern—History, Local. 5. Automobile travel—
California, Northern—Guidebooks. I. Maloof, Kathryn Golden. II.
Title.
F867.5.L585 2005
917.94'10454—dc22
2005014573

LIVING GOLD PRESS

P.O. Box 2
Klamath River, CA 96050
www.LivingGoldPress.com
jandk@livinggoldpress.com

CONTENTS

Fourth Printing Additions and Corrections

1. Roadside treasures continue to disappear at an alarming rate, including the **artifacts** pictured on the following pages: 115 (Shell sign), 128 (gas pumps), 135 (99 Motel sign), 167 (gas station), 170 (Snake Pit, partly there but hard to recognize--look for cactus), 176 (beer sign), 181 (classic neon signs), 193 (concrete overlayedby asphalt on Chestnut St.).

2. The freshly painted "**muffler man**" standing over an auto repair shop on old 99, north side of **Dunsmuir** (visible from I-5) is a recent addition. He was discovered face down in a wrecking yard (Dwight's, Crag View Dr., old 99) but his exact origins are unclear.

3. Page 120-121. The most recent **bridges at Gibson** were in fact not built until a major I-5 improvement project in the 1990s. The late 1950s freeway in this short stretch instead took a long curve off to the west. The curve was abandoned when the high bridges were built but the 1950s roadbed is visible from the present freeway.

4. Page 124, 196 and cover. **Dog Creek Bridge**. Access has been severely curtailed due to adjacent private property so you may have to enjoy it from underneath only (Fender's Ferry Rd. on west side of I-5, Vollmers Exit).

5. **Cottonwood** (P. 145) and **Cache Creek Bridges** (P.185) were torn down and replaced in 2004 (why?).

6. Remnants of pre-99 **Pacific Highway** circa 1912 continue to be discovered. Examples (north to south): A couple of **cement box culvert**-style bridges can be seen on the east side of I-5 between Hornbrook and Hilt in the **Bailey Hill Rd.** area. Near Weed, where **Truck Village Dr.** (old 99) ends, walk down the bank to the train track, look up to see a piece of cement road hanging off the far bank. Apparently the road was rerouted after this piece of track (Natron Cutoff) was laid (1926). One mile north of **Gibson** exit deep in a draw west of (and visible from) southbound I-5 is a **small old bridge over a creek** (large pullout with parking, but be careful). North of **Williams** on the east side of old 99 are other short segments and box culverts. A long cement-paved curve takes off about a mile north of Williams on the west side of old 99.

PREFACE
99

The road topped the crest of the Siskiyous, cut through a 4000' mountain pass chiseled out of solid rock, headed sharply downhill and south, and in a couple of miles crossed into a part of California sitting on the southern threshold of the conifer-covered Pacific Northwest. Over 900 miles later it ended in a sweltering desert valley on the border of another country. Inbetween, it bisected the State neatly into East and West. On its way south, it crossed mountain ranges, wound through tortuous river canyons, bee-lined across broad valleys dotted with magnificent oaks, passed through fertile fields and orchards, made its mark on innumerable settlements, large and small... This was Highway 99.

One of the three main north-south routes in the state, this was not the cool, coastal Highway 101 favored by romantics, nor the route claimed by isolated ranchers and desert rats, Highway 395. Highway 99 was the workingman's route, the most expedient way to traverse this long state, and along the way became the Main Street of the heart of California.

This story covers Highway 99 from the Oregon border to the state capital of Sacramento, a trip taking about five hours today. Yet it was an arduous, if not at times impossible trip to make in 1905, the year California first began registering automobiles. In that year, 2,475 cars were registered in the state. The cost was two dollars. Compare that to the more than 20 million registered today and it becomes clear how intrinsically entwined with driving is the modern California way of life.

The demand for good roads started just as soon as automobiles became more then a mere novelty. We consider it almost a basic right to be able to travel as quickly and safely as possible wherever and whenever we wish to go. How did we get to where we are today? Have we lost something in the journey?

My personal journey began about 1955 with several trips up and down the state on Highway 99. In the early fifties there was still the occasional steam engine plying the tracks north and south, although of course passenger trains were already well into their decline. My sister and I were young passengers in a forest green Ford Ranch Wagon. In my first clear memory of travel, I was peering in awe out of the rain-speckled back seat window of that heavy, spacious auto at the churning, lapping water while crossing the Yolo Causeway during the 1955 flood. We were heading to southern California for Christmas.

These trips were not exactly "fun," especially the summer-time ones. But they made an indelible impression on me, even at the age of three or four, that has stayed with me for over forty years. Stopping at a roadside stand for a cup of ice-cold cider or orange juice was a treat and necessity, and by nature much more refreshing than a Coke purchased at a McDonald's drive-up window from out of an air conditioned car.

Venture a short distance off of Interstate 5 onto a remnant of Highway 99 (and there are many) and you will find some faded vestiges of this bygone era: unique and beautifully designed old bridges; trunks of majestic oaks still barely flecked with the white paint that marked the road's curve; the empty shell of an old "Giant Orange" cafe. These things are so much more than man-made objects in various states of decay. They are windows into our recent past, a backward glimpse at a time not so long ago when life was at least seemingly simpler.

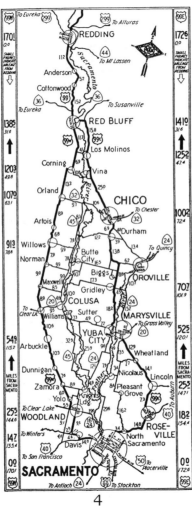

HIGHWAY EVOLUTION

All roads evolved in the same way, from footpath to wagon road to two-lane paved highway, and some to multi-laned super freeways. As automobiles increased in popularity, the demand for better roads, to make driving a more pleasurable and safer experience, rapidly increased. The yen to own a car spread swiftly. Horses were indescribably slow, no way to take a vacation. And Californians love to vacation. While one could travel on railroads, this limited mobility to where and when the trains would take you.

In fact, the advent of the automobile era was a great liberating force in California, and in the country as a whole.

In 1908 the Ford Model T went on sale for $850, with gasoline costing ten cents a gallon. It was billed as a "universal car," featuring simplicity and economy. The Model T displayed what might be considered "American" qualities. These were the first cars with a left side steering wheel. They were tough and hardworking. They were built high to scale deep ruts, built light for easy lifting out of the ruts.

The efficient assembly line method of manufacture that Ford pioneered kept the price of a Model T low. Within five years installment buying was initiated and the price dropped to $525. Suddenly automobile ownership was on the way to becoming an attainable goal for the average citizen.

Inspiration, Innovation

These coveted objects were rudimentary machines compared to what we drive today. They were slow, heavy, unheated, open to dust, mud, and insects, yet necessarily powerful in order to manage the deplorable roads. Things such as self-starters (eliminating the old crank start), electric lights, and detachable rims (allowing a tire to be changed rather than repaired on the spot) were all heralded as great innovations as they came along, as indeed they were.

A 1917 issue of *The California Motorist* carried the following item:

A contrivance patented and manufactured in San Francisco looking toward safety in automobile travel is now being put upon the market under the name of "The Diamond Stop and Turning Signal." The apparatus is simple, consisting of two small lamps attached to the rear of the car. Operated by a small switch it is possible to flash a red light on the right or left to indicate a right or left turn, while moving the switch to another notch flashes two red lights, indicating the intention of the driver to stop.

In a similar vein, many types of road improvement were painstakingly tried and accepted. Rough dirt or gravel roads, fine for wagon travel, quickly proved inadequate for "high speed" automobile traffic, and a little later, for heavy trucks, whose solid rubber tires tore up the soft surface. At first major rural roads were simply oiled in an attempt to keep the dust down, but this did little to alleviate the deep winter mud that made many roads virtually impassable.

Pavements were first developed for use on city streets, but such surfaces as stone or wood blocks were not practical for hundreds of miles of roadways. The arrival of the automobile era precipitated advancements beyond the broken stone or gravel of early "improved" rural roads. Concrete or macadam surfaces were experimented with, as finances allowed.

Completing the State Highway System would, theoretically at least, put an end to situations such as this on the Pacific Highway (later to become Highway 99) in Shasta County. The man on the right is Lester Gibson, a State Highway Engineer who during his long career played an important role in the transition of dirt roads into modern Highways. (Shasta Historical Society)

Macadam surfacing, one of the techniques borrowed from Europe, is named for a Scotsman, John MacAdam, who was instrumental in developing road building techniques in the early 1800s in England. A solid road base is built of compacted layers of uniformly sized gravel. It is then bound together with a stone dust-water mixture that forms a natural cement, and rolled for further compaction. A more durable variation was called tar macadam (thus "tarmac") in which the rock base was impregnated with tar, resulting in what we would call asphalt today.

Concrete was plentiful in California and was the most common surfacing material used on the Pacific Highway, the precursor to Highway 99. It was first laid out in a single narrow slab. When a wider road was called for, another slab could be easily poured alongside the first strip. And concrete has proven quite durable. In a few places you can still find remnants of concrete pavement pushing a century in age, even if some of them are now a patchwork of potholes and tar-filled cracks. (See *Where's the Concrete?* on Page 28)

The best surfacing material for each location, considering such factors as weather, terrain, and traffic conditions continues to be sought. At the same time lane width has grown ever wider. The earliest paved highways were generally only fifteen feet wide. Measure out that distance and then try to imagine driving on it with oncoming traffic! Twelve feet is the accepted width of one lane today.

There are other ways that the roadways evolved in their early years. White painted guard rails were put up in dangerous locations. Pneumatic tires were invented which resulted in less wear and tear of the road as well as a smoother ride.

Early roads were modernized in a process called "daylighting." The first highways followed the terrain of the land resulting in many sharp curves. The embankments were sometimes cut out ("daylighted") to improve visibility in a quick fix that would postpone the need for a new alignment.

Eventually lines were painted down the middle of the road to keep the two directions of traffic separate, as people tended to drive down the middle regardless of road width without them. The use of a broken stripe down the middle of the road didn't come into practice until the World War II years, in an effort that saved 110,000 gallons of paint and $200,000 in a single year.

All of the things we now take so much for granted required innovation and foresight, not to mention money, to become reality.

A HARDY BREED OF MEN

"These men maintained open highways in an era gone by. Damn little equipment and not alot of traffic, but these were the days of the beginning. These men didn't know any other duty than to keep the road open come hell or high water. They stayed on the job for long hours and I do mean long hours, they came home, wrung their long handles out, had a good drink of bootleg booze and went at it again. Their breed is gone and I mourn their passing. These are the men who paved the way for California State Employee Association and State Civil Service and I know they didn't even know the path they were pointing. I am sure glad I knew them."

The preceding comments are from a photo album showing highway maintenance of the twenties in the Mt. Shasta area compiled by N.E. Norton and now property of Sisson Museum. The tools and techniques of the day were amazingly primitive, yet they got the job done. Cracks in the pavement were sealed with hot tar poured by hand out of buckets. Next came the sand cart to cover the sticky substance. Before the cart arrived, it was a race for local children to grab a chunk of the pliant tar to be used as a no-cost chewing gum.

BIG DREAMS, LITTLE MONEY

Racing down the Interstate at more than a mile a minute, one seldom takes the time to wonder at the relative ease with which the miles roll by, to contemplate the highway and its evolution. We just want to get from Point A to Point B as rapidly and safely as possible. We expect to find the roads in excellent repair and the snow to be cleared immediately from mountain passes. As Californians, we are uniquely tied to our automobiles and consider excellent roads a given right. For the most part the State has met our wishes.

In the beginning, roads were haphazard and poorly planned, funded either locally by the county or privately (resulting in many toll roads and bridges). The success of the railroads in the late 1800s was partly at fault for the poor shape of the roads at the turn of the century. With railroad expansion, many established stage and freight routes fell into disrepair. Nobody wanted to pay for the necessary road maintenance.

But the State Legislature, ever concerned with the economic development of California, saw the wisdom of establishing a good road system as early as 1885. Their initial concern was the crossing of the Sierras near Lake Tahoe. The Lake Tahoe Wagon Road was purchased and became the first State Highway established by the three-member Bureau of Highways, the precursor of today's Caltrans, which was created over one hundred years ago in 1895.

The 17,000 Mile Road Trip

These newly appointed officials, engineers rather than the typical political appointees one might expect, proceeded to buy a buckboard wagon and team of horses, then travel nearly 17,000 miles throughout the state over the next two years. They found poor roads and a lack of order in their location. They even encountered traffic congestion on the narrow roads.

On returning, the Commissioners drew a map of their proposed state highway system which encompassed most of today's major routes. The proposed 14,000 mile system connected all population centers and all county seats, while utilizing already established roads when possible. The major north-south routes were called "trunk highways," these being connected by "laterals."

Then they began to study road building techniques; one Commission member traveled to Europe to study European methods. These men had foresight, but little money or power to back up their proposals.

Most of the meager amount of money earmarked for road work was provided by the counties, not the state, and went toward the more immediate needs of spring cleanup of debris left from winter storms, and constructing culverts, retaining walls, and bridges. Not much was left over for building good road bases and surfacing. Local governments exhibited varying degrees of enthusiasm toward these projects.

Road conditions must have provided a variety of surprises to motorists when traveling more than a few miles from home. For many years, the State Highway System was a dream with little financial backing.

Sketch Map
—or—
California.
OUTLINING THE STATE HIGHWAY SYSTEM
RECOMMENDED BY
THE BUREAU OF HIGHWAYS.
1896

In the first part of the century, the California Highway Commission marked their stock with this brand representing a "C", an "H", and a "C". Horses and mules, along with their human counterparts, provided all of the power in the early days of highway construction.

DAWN OF THE HIGHWAY ERA

By 1910, the public mood had changed. Automobile use had increased to the point where speeding, or "scorching" as it was then called, was now a problem. The public had to be instructed on the proper use of the horn. Driving clubs became popular, and the "Good Roads" movement spread. The fledgling California State Automobile Association formed a Good Roads Committee in Sacramento to push for favorable legislation.

In short cars, and trucks as well, were becoming such an integral part of the California lifestyle that we were now willing to start spending some money on our roads. A few people had attempted to stir up the public in favor of road development at the turn of the century. These included the League of American Wheelmen (bicyclists), who are credited with getting the first streets paved, it was the unstoppable increase of auto usage in the first decade of the twentieth century that provided the impetus for the legislation that was to follow.

In 1909 an act was passed by the California Legislature and approved by the people in the 1910 general election that finally made possible the real beginning of a unified system of state highways. This act provided for an $18,000,000 bond issue that would bring to reality the vision of the inspired, if essentially powerless, now defunct Bureau of Highways of fifteen years earlier. A new California Highway Commission was created within the Department of Engineering, which was responsible for actually acquiring rights-of-way and constructing the State Highway System. They had a tough job to do, considering the wildly varying terrain throughout the state, and the fact that some engineers estimated the cost would be a whopping thirty-five to fifty million dollars.

Another Trip

So another nearly seven thousand mile surveying trip was undertaken. One of the Commissioners describes the trip as follows;

We covered 6,850 miles in our tours. We were kicked off mountain roads by mules, we were stuck in river fords, we slid around dangerous mountain grades, we broke our windshield and punched holes in the bottom of our gasoline tank on the rocks on the desert, and after we had covered the trunk lines and laterals of California from Oregon to Mexico we went back to Sacramento and drew the State Highway routes on a big map of the state.

These men had the power and money that the first set of Commissioners lacked. Less than a year after the surveying trip, on August 7, 1912 (did government work faster in those days?) one of the Commissioners dug the first official shovelful of dirt on California State Highway Contract No. 1, a section of the Coast Highway south of San Francisco.

Interestingly, this in fact was **not** the first ground breaking on a State Highway. That had taken place with no fanfare at all a month earlier. Two workers held a mule-drawn plow as it bit into the earth three miles north of Wheatland on what would become Highway 99E.

It would be many years still before highways were given their familiar numerical designations. More poetically perhaps, roads were given names, a potential source of confusion at times no doubt when local variations came into play.

As a whole, what would become Highway 99 was known as the Pacific Highway (as opposed to the Pacific Coast Highway, 101) and it even had an association to promote it. The early twentieth century Pacific Highway Association headquartered in San Francisco visualized a continuous paved highway stretching all the way from the Canadian border to the Mexican border long before there was any money available or even effective state highway departments in place to implement the idea. It was supported by cities, counties and businesses.

In local usage, Highway 99 was generally known as the Pacific Highway from Sacramento north even long after it was given a number. South of Sacramento, it was known as the Golden State Highway or the Valley Route, and the Ridge Route or the Grapevine where it wound across the Tehachapis.

Since the dawning of the highway era, which we are likely to be in for the foreseeable future, highway design standards have been progressively raised to accommodate more traffic, higher speeds, heavier loads. This has resulted in more lanes, gentler grades, wider curves, and longer lasting and safer roads. Obviously a highway constructed at a time (1914) when there were only 126,000 cars in the state (as compared to over 20,000,000 today), and thirty five miles per hour was "putting the pedal to the metal," was built to lesser standards than a highway of the 1990s.

A straighter, wider road is an obvious sign of progress. Another less evident illustration of the evolving policies and philosophies behind the mundane task of road building is in the changing choices for bridge placement over the years.

In the early days of highway construction bridge sites were generally put at the narrowest part of the stream so the structure would be shorter and the foundation better. The highway was built wherever necessary in order to join the bridge. This practice was largely due to the high cost of bridge construction.

Yet this often resulted in dangerous curves at bridge approaches as well as longer highway distances.

In more recent construction, the best highway alignment has usually been determined first, and bridges were built more or less where they happened to fall. Shorter driving distances and straighter, safer alignments now take precedence over finances. Fewer curves, gentler grades, greater sight distances, smoother surfaces; safety and comfort—this is what highways are all about at the turn of the twenty-first century .

CHAPTER

4

MORE MONEY, QUICK

As should have been expected, the first $18 million was only a drop in the bucket. In 1913 an act was passed requiring all vehicles to be registered, the funds of which were to be used for highway maintenance. For the first time, a systematic system of highway maintenance could be implemented. The State Highway Act of 1915 provided for a $15 million dollar bond issue for highway construction, and not one county voted against it.

The insistence on high quality roads quickly ate up the highway funds. The Highway Commission had decreed that the new roads should be "permanent in character" and provide a "continuous and connected state highway system." Road width was to be fifteen feet in general and up to twenty feet in heavy traffic areas. The roads were good, but never were enough miles completed.

In 1919 Californians were anxious for the noticeable if slow progress on their highways to continue undeterred. The promise had been only partly realized, for at that time there was no strip of completed paved highway longer than thirty miles.

Meanwhile, in 1916 Congress had passed the Federal Aid Road Act. This first offer of federal funds for road construction was given with an eye to improving roads for rural mail delivery; thus the appellation "Post Roads." At that time in the nation as a whole there were three and a half million automobiles and half a million trucks as opposed to twenty one million horses, but the tide was beginning to turn.

The Federal Aid Road Act was a very significant event in highway history. The precedent of distributing federal monies for road construction planted the seed for the future US Highway System, of which Highway 99 was a part, and later the Interstate Highway System.

But for California to take part in the new program the Highway Commission had to come up with half of the costs. While it was successful in 1916 and 1917, California did not have the necessary $685,300 in 1919. So another $40,000,000 bond issue was passed in 1919 to provide for the required matching funds. The immediate goal was to complete the connecting links between the detached strips of highway.

Not surprisingly, the job still was not completed as planned. For one thing, World War I and its aftereffects made it difficult to sell all of the bonds. The

Cement was the first surfacing material used on State Highways, being poured here on Highway 99W near Corning in the first thrust of highway improvement in the mid-teens. (Caltrans)

dreamed of 14,000 mile road system had been reduced to a more realistic approximately 6,000 mile compromise, and still not even a third of the proposed mileage had a permanent hard surface by the early 1920s.

There were also problems of maintenance and even rebuilding. The earliest highways were paved in concrete poured directly on the ground, a job that required muscle power of both man and beast. The Department owned their own horses and mules in the early years. Animals pulled the wagons of gravel from the borrow pit, pulled the scraper for grading the roadbed, pulled the mixer into position. Men wheeled the cement in wheelbarrows and finished it with a plank fitted to plow handles. On a good day, 150 feet of road were paved.

What an embarrassment to the Highway Commission when the beautiful new cement roads in the Central Valley began to crumble due to water seeping in from roadside rice paddies. And as heavy trucks took to the roads the hard-won miles of smooth pavement took a beating. New techniques had to be learned. The State was helped in such matters by the increasingly active automobile clubs, particularly the Automobile Club of Southern California, which did technical research and made recommendations to the Commission.

Some money was saved by using convict labor to build roads, generally in remote areas where labor was scarce. But it wasn't long before it was recognized that another method of financing the ambitious highway projects would be necessary. In 1923 a two cent gasoline tax was introduced. This funding method was here to stay, the rate creeping up until today we pay state gasoline tax, federal tax, and state sales tax on gasoline totaling nearly half the price of a gallon of gas.

Throughout the years our highway system was being so aggressively established, more miles were periodically added to the system. Naturally, it was an ongoing effort to keep the highways up to the expected high standards, but by 1930 the major highways were well under control. So the thrust of the 1930s was embodied in the slogan, "Get the Farmer Out of the Mud": that is, improvement of the secondary, so called "farm to market" roads.

Over time the Highway Commission of such humble beginnings became an increasingly more powerful entity, evolving into the Division of Highways of the Public Works Department, and then the California Department of Transportation, known today as Caltrans.

Where's the Concrete?

Concrete was the first type of pavement used on Highway 99 starting way back in 1912. The pavement was generally poured in a 15' wide strip. Sometimes another strip was laid alongside the first to widen the highway. Amazingly, a few remnant patches can still be found. Here are some northern California concrete treasures:

- Chestnut St. in Mt. Shasta City

- another small piece off Mt. Shasta Blvd. near the Humane Society

- Redding on N. Boulder Dr.

- Anderson on Barney Rd.

- Red Bluff in front of Hess Bros. wrecking yard

- W. Sacramento on Tower Ct. near Tower Bridge approach

- several in southern California—see *That Ribbon of Highway II*

MOTORING, A CALIFORNIA PASTIME

In the first decades of the twentieth century, trains were an important part of everyday life. Automobiles and highway travel seeped their way gradually into the California consciousness. The process was similar throughout the nation, but given its great size, widely separated cities, unique and beautiful physical features inviting exploration, and free-spirited population, Californians most enthusiastically embraced the automobile and the freedom it embodied. By 1929, California had the highest per capita vehicle registration in the country.

What did automobile ownership mean in the early part of the century? Government regulation first reared its head in 1905 with the introduction of automobile registration, although it was not yet required. At this time each owner was issued a round brass disc to keep on the dashboard, but he had to make his own license plates. Consequently they were made of various materials, even leather. In 1914, after registration became mandatory, the State issued porcelain plates. Steel was first used in 1920.

Car owners or not, everyone experienced changes in the commercial landscape as a result of automobiles and highways. Stables, blacksmiths, and hitching posts began to disappear. New enterprises took their places, such as garages, gas stations, hot dog stands, auto camps, even gypsy fortune tellers and other gimmicky, tourist oriented businesses. Small towns lost some of their importance as travel to larger towns to work or to shop became easier. In the early part of the century, the automobile, in combination with radio and motion pictures, brought disconnected people and places closer together in the state and the country as a whole.

The horse era was waning, the automobile era waxing. In 1917 the city of Los Angeles announced that it was considering closing its three main business streets to horse-drawn traffic. Yet long distance automobile travel was still a challenge not to be taken lightly. Mud, steep grades, and continual breakdowns had to be contended with. Car travel vied with train travel for dominance for decades.

Californians (and other Americans) were inexorably drawn to automobile travel for a variety of reasons, such as the perceived or real freedom, romance, style, and convenience embodied in driving a car. A number of promotional activities did their part to plant the seeds of desire in the American public.

Highly publicized transcontinental automobile trips were attempted, the first successful trip taking place in 1903. The trip took sixty-four days. Delays were caused by difficulty in obtaining gas and oil, and the frequent necessity of using block and tackle to pull the car out of mud.

Other publicity trips were undertaken over the years. A large caravan of cars (this one sponsored by the manufacturers of Premier Automobiles) crossed the country and ended dramatically right in the surf at Los Angeles in 1911. A 1912 transcontinental motor-truck trip demonstrated the suitability of transporting cargo by truck. Soon cross country trips were so commonplace as to be hardly worth mentioning.

An auto race from Los Angeles to Sacramento with nineteen participants took place in 1914. The winner averaged forty miles per hour, crediting his success to the fact that he went the entire distance without a flat tire.

Following World War I in 1919, the U.S. Army sent a truck caravan across the country to demonstrate the feasibility of long distance motor transportation, and to investigate the desirability of federal highway aid. The states were given surplus military trucks for use in highway maintenance. The California Highway Commission created the new position of Equipment Engineer to select and distribute the excess war goods. The mules were definitely on their way out.

The Panama-Pacific International Exposition, the world's fair held in San Francisco in 1915 to celebrate the opening of the Panama Canal, was another catalyst for road improvement in Northern California. Since people from all over the world would be traveling to California, there was a widespread effort to spruce things up, including the roads, to give the state a modern, progressive appearance.

In addition, one exhibit at the fair proved to be irresistible to fair goers. Ford Motor Company installed a working automobile assembly plant in the Palace of Transportation. Eighteen cars, or one every ten minutes, were built every afternoon. There were forty other automobile exhibits at the fair. What a demonstration of the arrival of the Automobile Era!

Hard Travelin', But With a Guide

Even with all of the publicity and enthusiasm, good roads were slow in coming. But travel Californians did, often with the help of a guidebook, for the way was not always direct and the road signs few. One of the earliest of these is *Thorpe's Illustrated Road Map and Tour Book of California 1911*. Printed in the long, narrow format typical of the era (to fit easily in the glove box?), the book provides a rare insight into travel in the early part of the century. As stated on the cover, it shows "actual photos of the location of turns, forks, cross roads, landmarks, hotels, resorts, inns, points of interest, with much supplementary information to motorist and tourist."

The tiny photos do indeed show things such as "sign at fork," "pump at branch," and "stable at turn," for this is how early motorists navigated in the absence of road signs. The accompanying maps detail the road mile by mile,

This classic service station and garage along Highway 99 in Dunsmuir was probably a local hang out as well as a stopping point for motorists. As automobile traffic increased, so did the businesses to meet the traveler's needs. (Siskiyou County Museum)

with all bridges, washes, summits, ferry crossings, railroad crossings, ditches, gas stations, and hotels noted.

Included is a page depicting common road signs, with the warning that "in many places they are defaced, while others are missing, but they are useful and correct where they exist." Additionally there is a page of "Auto Laws" summarizing the "Gist" of Los Angeles and San Francisco laws. ("Turn full corners, give up half the road." "Must have gong or horn." "No sirens, claxons, cut outs, or other disagreeable sounds permitted.")

Road surfaces and percent grade are noted in this and other guidebooks of the era. The Fireman's Fund Insurance Company published one in 1921. Printed alongside the maps are such hints as "Fair mountain road. Many sharp curves. Hotels and garages at all principal towns. Fireman's Fund Agents at all principal towns." (Well, of course!)

In short, a traveler starting off on a road trip in the early days was well advised to be armed with a guidebook or at least one of the cloth-mounted road maps of the day to make the going easier and safer.

Things changed rapidly in the following decades. While the original routes generally followed the natural lay of the land, as road building technology advanced and roads were improved, they appeared higher up the slopes above the streams in mountainous areas. Larger road cuts, higher bridges, and gentler grades were the result.

At the same time, motorists acquired the taste of freedom that driving an automobile affords. Californians were on the move! And in 1929 the Highway Patrol was organized to make sure they weren't moving too fast.

Auto Camps, Auto Courts, and Motels

When the shadows start to lengthen at the end of the day, the highway traveler begins to wonder, "Where will we stay tonight?" The answer to that question changed over the years along with the growing popularity of traveling in a car and the evolution of the highways and the automobiles themselves.

At the turn of the century overnight accommodations consisted of either hotels in a city, small town male-oriented drummer's (traveling salesmen's) hotels, or resorts in scenic areas usually reached by train, all requiring the formal modes of dress and social decorum that this new type of tourist sought to escape. Motorists too would occasionally stay in these places, but the automobile traveler was generally of a different temperament; a little more adventurous, anxious to explore where the vehicle would take him, unwilling to stay put in one spot for a week or two at a time, as was the custom at the resorts.

As middle class families rushed to tour the countryside in their new cars during the second decade of the twentieth century, the term "gypsying" was used to describe the emerging style of travel that featured a route, destination, and timetable of the motorists'choice, and roadside camping. The old style resorts gradually faded as automobile travel flowered, and urban hotels catered to another crowd.

The large old cars could carry quite an array of gear and supplies. Auto campers loved gadgets. As gypsying gained popularity, tents, folding beds, and other specially designed camping gear proliferated. Tent sales reached a peak in 1923-24. Motorists declared their independence from the constraints of society (at least until their return to work and home a week or two in the future) by the proud display of tin cans mounted on the car's radiator. What held last night's dinner was turned into a light hearted symbol of defiance.

Unfortunately, favored camping spots quickly became overused and littered. Motorists had conflicts with nearby farmers. Towns along the highways were unhappy that these "gypsy" travelers were spending very little money in their towns.

Before long, the first type of formalized accommodations geared specifically to the motorist crowd were created. These municipal parks, or "auto camps," were built in or on the edge of the highway towns. The towns initially provided the auto camps free of charge in hopes of luring the motorist trade to local stores, gas stations, and cafes. Often there was fierce competition between rival towns to provide the best facilities. Comparing various auto camps up and down the highway was a favorite campfire topic. Word spread fast on the gypsy grapevine.

This well-preserved auto court, complete with car ports, was built on Highway 99 in Redding about sixty years ago. Once known as the Hidalgo Courts, the facility has evolved into a small apartment complex and no longer serves the traveling public.

The town of Corning on Highway 99 is credited with having the first auto camp in California, opening in 1900 in an olive grove. This camp had electricity, cement wash tubs, and shady trees to park under.

Inevitably, a free campground with amenities such as hot showers and central kitchens attracted impoverished travelers and transients. Local enthusiasm for the free auto camps faded. To keep out the "undesirables," small fees were generally imposed by 1920.

Charging fees opened up the field to private enterprise. A farmer along a major highway could set up camping spots, build some tent platforms, maybe put in a gas pump, even a small store or cafe, and be in business. The result was more selection and better services for the auto campers.

By the mid twenties motorists appear to have lost some of their rebellious spirit. They tired of carrying all that camping equipment. Tent sales plummeted. Auto camp owners responded by turning tent platforms into simple cabins, but you still needed to bring your own bedding and cooking gear. Bathrooms were communal (as they still were in most hotels of the era). This signaled the raw beginnings of the motel industry. The rebel "gypsies" who a decade before sought simplicity and self-sufficiency were turning into comfort-loving consumers.

The humble cabins in the auto camps were quickly upgraded, if the place hoped to stay in business. Good beds, linens, and indoor plumbing were added. The cabins were comfortable enough to attract former hotel patrons during the Depression. Non-campers came to recognize the advantages of easy access, no reservations, no tipping, informality, and fresh air just outside your door. To disassociate themselves from their lowly beginnings these establishments, called "auto courts," were the direct forerunners of what came to be known as "motels." This term originated in California and gained national acceptance after World War II when it first appeared in English dictionaries. Motel, a combination of "motor" and "hotel" at first written as "mo-tel," was coined in 1926 to name a rather fancy Spanish mission style auto court in San Luis Obispo, California.

Seventy years later, the distinction between an expensive motel and a hotel is blurry, and "campgrounds" accommodate vehicles that cost as much as a house.

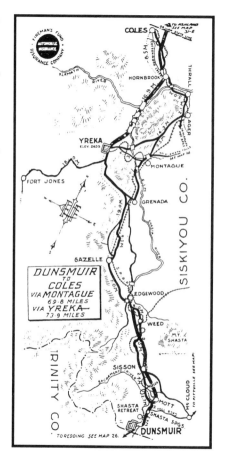

Map from Automobile Tour Book of California, *Fireman's Fund Insurance of California, 1921.*

FROM AUTO CAMP TO MOTEL

The Cave Springs Motel in Dunsmuir has a history that spans the range of the changing expectations of motorists looking for a place to stay. Although it now features a pool, HBO, a spa and RV spaces, it was only a humble campground with showers and toilets when it opened in 1922.

But the owners were quick to adapt. In 1925 they built some California box-type cabins (i.e., no studs, no insulation) and tent platforms. Hot water was provided by a huge wood-fired boiler. The sooty grime put out by steam engines passing on the nearby tracks called for continual cleaning.

The place was a haven for travelers, especially residents of the scorching Central Valley craving cool mountain air in the summertime. The motel's changing appellation, from "Brown's Auto Camp" to "Brown's Auto Park" to "Brown's Modern Motel Lodge" to "Cave Springs Motel," is indicative of the changing times and how the owners kept up with them. Some of the original cabins are still in use.

The current owner, who grew up on the grounds of Cave Springs in the fifties, remembers well the thundering trucks roaring by on Highway 99 just a few feet in front of his family's motel, and the fatal accident that hastened the building of the freeway that now bypasses Dunsmuir.

The photograph shows Brown's Auto Park in the mid to late twenties.(Louie Dewey)

HIGHWAY 99 IS BORN

By the 1920s it was evident that a standardized system of designating the major highway routes that were spreading so rapidly across the nation was needed. The haphazard method of locally named roads would no longer suffice. "Trail associations" had capitalized on the public's need for designated and signed popular routes by doing some signing and mapping to bring a little order into the chaos, but the effort was piecemeal and insufficient. Some of these groups unscrupulously collected fees from members and gave nothing in return. Eventually, a national group known as the American Association of State Highway Officials stepped in.

With their billboards adorning the highway all the way up the north state and their hard-to-forget name, everyone knew about the Crook's Brothers Service Station "on the curve" in Corning. (Corning Museum)

Two Crooks

Selling Gas

SOUTH ENTRANCE TO CORNING

Camp in Orange Grove

All Modern Conveniences

CROOK'S BROS SERVICE STATION

This group generated our current method of designating highways by number in a routine manner when the need for a more uniform method became evident. And so, in 1926 Highway 99 as we know (or knew) it came into being when the US Highway System was established. The goal was to bring in 3% of a state's road miles under the US umbrella.

Thus this long highway that traversed the entire state of California, a work-in-progress that had been visualized thirty years previously, was finally given its famous number designation, with a "US" in front. Now the entire route, from Mexico to Canada, was united under the "99" symbol and signed with US Highway shields.

Under the new US system, north-south routes were given odd numbers (lowest numbers in the east) and east-west routes were given even numbers (lowest numbers in the north), with a few exceptions. So, the north-south US

Highways ranged from US1 along the east coast to US101 along the west coast.

Lateral highways connecting the major routes were to retain the major route's number with a third digit added at the beginning. These three-digit highways could be viewed as "children" of the major routes. Highway 299, a lateral route heading east and west from Redding, is an offspring of Highway 99. There was also a provision for alternate routes off of the main route. And so we had both a 99E and a 99W between Red Bluff and Sacramento.

That isn't to say that the descriptive names instantly fell into disuse. The public persists with the colorful names to this day. Even maps were slow to recognize the new number designations.

Signs and Shields

At the same time that the numbers were being passed out, the familiar white shield with black numbers, known as the United States Shield, was the style of official highway sign picked to adorn these major highways of the Federal Aid Road System. Yet the State was still unwilling or unable to spend any money on the much needed signing effort. This job was undertaken by two of the automobile clubs. Starting in 1928, the California State Automobile Association placed signs in the forty five northern counties, and the Automobile Club of Southern California did the same in the thirteen southern counties.

It should be noted that this numbering system applied to roads in the U.S.

The two nines on what was known as the United States Shield were embellished with round reflectors. This style of sign was adopted in the mid-twenties for use on highways in the Federal Aid Road System, at the same time that highways were given their number designations and Highway 99 officially came into being. Initially the numbers on the sign were squared. These rounded numbers were used in the forties and fifties.

Highway System only; that is, routes receiving federal funds, of which Highway 99 was one. Most of these routes also crossed more than one state (as 99 crosses California, Oregon, and Washington on its way from Mexico to Canada) resulting in a plethora of confusing local names that made a simple number more practical, if less appealing. The U.S. Highway System was the forerunner of Eisenhower's Interstate Highway System.

California quickly jumped on the bandwagon, numbering non-Federal Aid State Highways in the same orderly manner, while carefully avoiding duplication of any of the U.S. Highway numbers. The automobile clubs took on these signing responsibilities as well. State Highways were adorned with the "bear shield," shaped like a miner's spade and displaying a grizzly bear above the number. Signs on local roads were black on white rectangles incorporating a small automobile club logo. In 1934, the Division of Highways belatedly assumed the road signing duties.

However, the State of California continued to identify different portions of 99 and other US Highways with their own numbers. The result being that a section of highway could conceivably have three different assigned numbers: a US Highway number, a State Route number, and a State Legislative Route number. What a source of confusion when looking at old maps! Maybe naming the highways was the best idea after all.

Don't Leave Home Without It

Even after the roads were denoted and signed, the early to mid-century automobile traveler was still likely to use a guidebook. Today, many a driver might enter the freeway at a given on ramp and literally not stop or even look more than a few feet to his right or left until he reaches his destination hundreds of miles later. Sadly, few travelers seem to exhibit much interest in what treasures lie off to the sides of the freeway.

Motorists in the not-too-distant past considered traveling a journey as much as a destination. Perhaps some of this sentiment was imposed by the relatively primitive technology of the day (slower cars, no air conditioning, etc.) Whatever the reasons, traveling seems to have been slower paced, more fulfilling, if more difficult.

Wordy, mile-by-mile guidebooks full of sightseeing gems were common until the early sixties. The earliest guidebooks actually helped the travelers find their way along the often unmarked highway, letting them know not only where to turn but also where to find gasoline or lodging. Later books told more about road conditions (type of surfacing, percent grade), and described the towns along the highways as well as the sightseeing and recreational opportunities. By the late twenties it was no longer necessary to worry about where to gas up or where to stay, for automobile travel had become so entrenched that roadside businesses were everywhere.

Trains Versus Cars

It is interesting to note the competition between train and automobile travel as exhibited in these guidebooks. The first generation of motorists had been raised on train travel. At the turn of the century, a strictly followed railroad timetable seemed to represent the American mastery over outside factors such as bad weather and rough terrain. Motoring was a step backwards in comfort but the freedom it embodied was intoxicating, addictive. Public disillusion with train travel increased during World War I when freight and troops preempted civilian passengers. The switch to car travel took place gradually over more than half a century.

Rider's California, published in 1928, focuses on the railroad. Train stops are mentioned first. Where the highway and rail routes diverge, towns on the "Pacific Highway" are mentioned secondarily. A 1939 guide gives both modes of transportation fairly equal billing.

By the fifties, highways are clearly dominant, trains barely mentioned in the guidebooks. Thumbing through *Sunset Magazines* from the early fifties reveals a plethora of advertisements for all modes of transportation. Representative of their imminent decline, the fewer, smaller railroad ads stress the scenic, relaxing quality of train travel. In other ads the newcomer airlines, are just starting to come into their own emphasizing speed, of course, (although it took about nine hours to fly across the country) and even comfort, for those early airliners came equipped with beds and private cabins for long flights!

Cars are clearly in the forefront with every kind of automobile, automobile accessory, gasoline, and motor oil lavishly displayed to hopefully entice Californians to purchase the products. But items once considered luxuries are now necessities. It takes no advertising to get us to buy a tank of gas or quart of oil.

In those heady post-war days of four or five decades ago service stations, whose crude beginnings consisted of a drum, a bucket, and a funnel kept behind the general store, were in fact "service stations." As the back of a 1950 Chevron California road map proclaims, "We always clean windshields for safer vision...check oil and water, fan belt, and other danger spots. Tell us you have a spare minute and we'll also inspect tires for correct pressure, check battery. Count on us, too, for helpful travel information and shining clean restrooms."

WPA Guides

When we started our 99 research in the mid-1990s the first place we went was to our local library. And the first thing we found was the WPA guide, *California*, part of the American Guide Series. And what a treasure we had found!

California is a weighty tome of over 700 pages with a fold-out state highway map inserted in the back. It was first published in 1939, the result of the collaboration of numerous unnamed and heretofor unemployed writers during the Great Depression.

The Writer's Project was an offshoot of the Works Project Administration of Roosevelt's New Deal. The 48 state guides and several city guides published were a major achievement. For a good twenty years at least the guides were immeasurably helpful to motorists traveling along one of the designated tours, such as "Tour 3" in the book *California*, "US 99 from the Oregon Line to the Mexican Border." The richness of the chapters on such subjects as local history, industry, and architecture had never been found in guidebooks before.

The newly employed writers fanned out across the country, from big city to hamlet, and recorded their impressions in descriptive prose. Their words are a mirror of our country as it then was, sandwiched between two world wars, in all of its amazing variety and complexity.

CHAPTER

7

SEEKING THE 99 TRAIL

The "99" traveler of the early to middle 1900s underwent a journey that is difficult for us to imagine or to remember, as the case might be. It is another kind of challenge to follow in their footsteps today. If our goal is to travel as closely as possible the route of "Old 99" and much of it is unmarked or indiscernible, where is it? Where has it gone?

Or even, which "99" is it? For in most areas the alignment changed over the years as the highway was improved. The 99 shields went up on the newer road and the former "99" was either buried, abandoned or transferred to local control.

Thus the search for the old highway is something of a detective game, much like piecing together a puzzle. Keep in mind that there were basically three versions of 99. Pieces of all three can still be found. The final version was the freeway version. As sections of US99 were gradually brought up to freeway status at various times from the late 1950s onward, the "99" designation was replaced by an "I-5" designation.

The original north-south route of what was to become Highway 99 was either built or improved upon (using already existing roads) in the first thrust of State Highway construction, from 1911

Following the 99 trail often leaves you on a piece of abruptly ending piece of old highway, such as this spot on what is now called Mott Airport Rd. The relatively straight line of the Interstate cuts across the curvy configuration of Highway 99, leaving fragments of the old road isolated on either side.

to 1915. This Pacific Highway, as it was called, is the most obscure; much of it is long gone. This was the concrete pavement era. Or even the no-pavement era, for a good portion of this road through the mountainous areas was never paved.

The version of Highway 99 that was constructed in the mid-twenties and periodically renovated until the inception of Interstate 5 is the road with which we are most familiar. This is the pre-freeway highway that many of us remember driving or riding along in our youth.

To build this second "99" the curves of the original state highway from the teens were straightened, the grades reduced, the roadbed widened, and the highway officially became US99 (in 1926.) This road survives in scattered but intact bits and pieces throughout the north state.

Such as in the flat Sacramento Valley, where long stretches of old Highway 99 endure and even retain their 99 label (although of course the "99" no longer refers to a US Highway.) Here, the construction challenges that highway engineers had to meet were fewer. Without mountains, rocks, slides, gorges, or steep gradients to contend with, when the old road proved inadequate it was a relatively simple matter to widen it. Little dirt had to be moved or rocks blasted or depressions filled. In other instances a new highway was constructed adjacent to the old. The original road remained in use for local traffic.

Today, freeway frontage roads are often portions of the old highway, even outside of the valley. In the more mountainous areas, a familiar sight along the 99 trail is a yellow "END" sign, where a disconnected and unidentified section of the old highway is abruptly cut off at the very edge of a swath of the freeway that replaced it. The relatively straight, wide strip of Interstate 5 slices across the more acute twists and turns of old Highway 99, isolating fragments on either side of the freeway and burying the rest. Abrupt ends are a good sign that you've found, and just reached the end of, a piece of the old highway.

And so the several 99s are overlapped, intersected, subsumed, abandoned, renamed, cut off, and ignored in varying degrees. This is where the detective work (and fun) comes in.

CONSTRUCTION CHALLENGES

Building the highway across the flatlands of northern California was generally trouble free. It was mostly a matter of obtaining the necessary funds and determining the best surfacing material. By 1920, just a few years into the State Highway program, Highway 99 was paved as far north as Red Bluff.

However, constructing in the mountainous regions was another matter. Paving was the very least of the problems. The earliest version of the highway was built along the path of least resistance, generally following the natural contours of the land. Keep in mind the primitive aspect of the tools and methods in those early days of highway construction; shovels, wheelbarrows, and horse drawn scrapers as opposed to today's mammoth earth movers and dump trucks.

Naturally this resulted in many miles of travel to cover the short distance between two points. Where the first rendering of the highway might sideslope lengthily all around the edges of a canyon, later versions would cross the same canyon on deep fill or a tall bridge, cutting off miles of travel.

The original highway went steeply up and down slopes where the natural contours could not be followed. In later years, when blasting or digging out huge chunks of mountainside and disposing of the material became feasible, this was done.

The main goals in road improvement were, and continue to be, shorter distances, more gradual grades, straighter roads, safety. Two geographical areas in particular, both in mountainous regions, presented the highway engineers with numerous difficulties to overcome in achieving these goals.

CONQUERING THE SHASTA RIVER CANYON

Up near the Oregon border, between Yreka and the Klamath River, Highway 99 was carved into the side of the Shasta River canyon. This canyon is a rugged, spectacular piece of topography; the surrounding scenery a juniper-studded moonscape. The completion of the highway through here in 1931 was considered an engineering triumph. The showpieces, besides the surrounding terrain, are the five bridges crossing the Shasta and Klamath Rivers, the middle three in particular. They lost some of their charm in a 1970s refurbishing project, but are still worth a closer look. This portion of old Highway 99 has been rechristened Highway 263.

The original north-south stage route avoided this rough canyon with its inherent problems and followed a track several miles to the east. When it came time to lay out the route for the new State Highway through this region in 1912, the question of location was faced. The canyon route was obviously the most direct way to head up over the Siskiyous and the connection with Oregon's Rogue Valley, but tackling it would be difficult and expensive. Thus the favored route was off to the east, bypassing Yreka, the county seat.

But the canyon route had its advocates, no doubt many of them Yrekans rightfully concerned about the possible demise of their town if the other route were chosen. Whether the decision was political or not isn't recorded, but the Shasta Canyon route was eventually chosen. Oddly, a similar scenario was played out over fifty years later when the routing of Interstate 5 was being planned, and again Yreka came out the winner.

And so nine and a half new miles of State Highway were constructed in 1914, from just north of Yreka to beyond where the Shasta spills into the Klamath River and the Klamath River Highway to the coast begins. The new highway contained 137 curves, some of them "hairpin" (defined as having a fifty foot or less radius), with a maximum grade of 7%. As severe as this might seem now, at the time the completion of this road was considered a remarkable accomplishment. Why, it was so wide (16 feet!) that two directions of traffic were possible at the same time! Speeds of up to thirty miles an hour could be reached, and guard rails protected the dangerous curves.

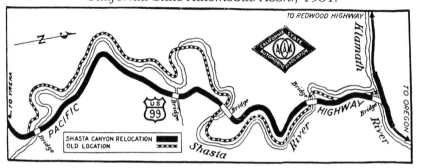

California State Automobile Assn., 1931.

Remnants of this first unpaved highway lie far below the present road (Highway 263), down by the river. Much of it can be driven on today, providing excellent views of the highway and bridges built in the next phase of highway construction.

In only a decade this acclaimed highway was already obsolete. It was too steep, windy, and dangerous for the rapidly increasing traffic of the twenties but the nature of the gorge prevented a quick fix.

A new alignment for this section of the Pacific Highway (later called US Highway 99), one removed from the narrow confines of the canyon bottom, was planned during the next thrust of State Highway construction in the mid-twenties. The choice was between a road high up the slopes with bridges cutting across the canyons, or a somewhat lower road that would necessitate the construction of several tunnels. The high road was chosen.

A philosophical change was in the works, no doubt due to the pressure of rapidly increasing traffic and supported by the revenue the 1923 gasoline tax provided, in which safety and shortened distances justified large expenditures of money. Five bridges were built in four and a half miles of this road, making this the most thickly bridged section of any part of California's highway system at the time. 240 tons of explosives were used in the excavation.

Two of the bridges are of the graceful concrete arch style that was commonly built in that time period, and are indisputably beautiful. The open sides of all the bridges and the built-in benches on the concrete arch over Dry Gulch were unfortunately filled in during the aforementioned "improvements" of the late seventies. The middle bridge, known as the Pioneer Bridge, is a long steel cantilever structure. The bridges can best be appreciated when viewed from below, on portions of the original, canyon-bottom highway.

Thus another portion of Highway 99 was complete. The road was shortened by two miles. The number of curves was reduced to only twenty five and the grade to four percent. *Motorland,* the California State Automobile Association publication, called it "a momentous chapter in the progress of California's highway development." The dedication was held in August of 1931 on the Pioneer Bridge. It was attended by local pioneers and the governors of both California and Oregon, as befitting this crucial link between the two states.

When Interstate 5 came through the area in 1970, the canyon route was rejected as being completely unsuitable to house a modern four-lane freeway. This section of Highway 99 lost its venerable number and the majority of its traffic. But locals heading down to the Klamath River use it daily, and when the snow flies, truckers prefer this route to the freeway's steep climb over Anderson Grade.

BRIDGE TALK

Bridges are enduring monuments to the legacy of the early highway era. Even a casual traveler can't fail to note these important structures that so ably link the pieces of roadway separated by rivers, streams, canyons and gorges. Just what is their history, and how did bridges change in form and function as the 20th century unfolded?

At the turn of the century road travel was by horse and wagon. The wagon roads were just beginning to be improved a little for motor vehicle usage. The road was long but practicable to build and maintain; deep canyons were bypassed and water crossings kept to a minimum.

In spite of lengthy detours, sooner or later obstacles had to be met. Streams were forded if small enough. Ferries crossed rivers. Crude log bridges were constructed across larger streams. In unforested locations that yielded no logs for building material, hewn timbers were brought in to construct wooden trestle style bridges.

Wooden truss bridges with their triangular framework were a slightly more sophisticated bridge form. Sometimes these were made into covered bridges with the addition of roof and siding for greater longevity, especially where the climate was wet.

Suspension bridges were another early bridge type. Entrepreneur A.S. Halladie of San Francisco experimented with uses for the wire cable he manufactured and came up wire cable suspension bridges (as well as his famous cable cars) in the 1860s.

Many of these early structures were hastily built by private parties who charged a toll for usage, of course. Many met their demise at the hands of high water or heavy loads. Others, built as they were of a dry, flammable material, succumbed to fire. The initial effort to keep barrels full of water on every wooden bridge soon proved impractical.

Thorpe's Illustrated Auto Road Map of 1911 shows that the route from Sacramento to the Oregon border which later became Highway 99, had numerous bridges in place at that time, excepting the Sacramento River crossing at Redding and the Pit River crossing a few miles north. In these two places the traveler took fifty cent ferry rides.

As we have seen, the struggling Division of Highways was constantly strapped for funds in the early years. In its effort to get the State Highway System rolling, the State requested that individual counties be responsible for the bridges needed along the State Highways routes. This worked well for a time, if at a slower pace than the Commissioners would have liked.

Thus during the first period of State Highway construction in the teens, the vast majority of bridges were designed and built by county road departments. One still standing exception is the small concrete girder bridge with pipe railings crossing Shotgun Creek. This bridge is on a narrow piece of old highway in the canyon a few miles south of Dunsmuir. It was built in 1915, one of the few bridges that remain from that era actually designed by State Highway Engineers rather than county surveyors or county-hired consulting bridge engineers. For that reason, despite its rather humble appearance, it was given historical status and must remain in place.

Inevitably, the State tired of waiting for the counties to complete the necessary bridges. In 1923, with the assured funding of the new gasoline tax, the State took over all of the bridge design and construction responsibilities. And so began an epoch of creative bridge design.

Early in the century, after wooden structures fell out of favor, many highway bridges were of the boxy yet functional metal (steel or iron) truss design, a carryover from the railroad era. In fact these bridges, which could be ordered out of catalogs in standard designs, were manufactured by the same bridge companies that built similarly styled railroad bridges. Some actually were recycled train bridges. In highway usage, metal trusses were often built to minimal standard. The lightly braced structures were commonly known as howlers, rattlers, or squeakers.

When the changing sensibilities of the teens and twenties tagged the utilitarian truss bridges as "ugly" in the public mind, reinforced concrete gradually became the material of choice. Besides, concrete was plentiful in California and steel was expensive. Californians pioneered the use of concrete in bridge construction. The nation's very first reinforced concrete bridge was built way back in 1888 and still stands in San Francisco's Golden Gate Park.

Early county-built concrete bridges were merely plain and serviceable. Soon enough, form and function would meet in the beautifully designed concrete bridges that flourished in the early days of State designed and built highway bridges.

This period was inspired and presided over by State Bridge Engineer Harlan D. Miller, who insisted on handsome structures down to the details of railings and endposts. He favored structures that would enhance a grand natural setting.

Wooden "falsework" was used in constructing the concrete arch that spans the Sacramento River at Dunsmuir, completed in 1916. The bridge is still in use, carrying half of Interstate 5 on its deck. (Caltrans)

He realized that attractive structures belong on the rural byways as well as in big cities. Under his tutelage numerous stately bridges were built, particularly concrete arches, throughout the 1920s and 1930s. In fact concrete arch designs, some of them patented, came to be identified nationwide with California's State Highway System. The concrete arch that still spans Dog Creek in the Sacramento River Canyon (although no longer in use) was named after Mr. Miller when it was completed soon after his death in 1927. This structure is historically significant and will not be demolished, unless by vandals.

A surprising number of the old highway bridges are intact, left in place when the road was rerouted. Others were modified for modern traffic conditions, such as the arch built in 1916 at Dunsmuir that still carries one half of Interstate 5, and the bridges over Doney and Charlie Creeks on Lakeshore Dr. with their decks raised to accommodate man-made Shasta Lake.

Others were blown up in the name of progress, at the hands of the U.S. Army personnel who were given the opportunity to practice their demolition skills on obsolete structures.

One exception to this practice was on Highway 99's Pit River crossing north of Redding. The ferry was put out of business in 1916 with the completion of the 242-foot concrete arch that for many years was the longest concrete span in the state. When the new dual purpose automobile/train bridge was finished in 1942, the original arch was judged to be too close to the immense concrete pilings of the new bridge for safe demolition. So the intact 1916 Pit River bridge slowly disappeared beneath the rising waters of Shasta Lake, perhaps for future underwater archeologists to someday explore.

The freeway-era bridges we speed across today even while barely cognizant of their existence are undoubtedly marvels of engineering. But at least in the eyes of the casual traveler, these modern structures exhibit a bland, generic quality, if they're noticed at all...

LOIS' BIG ADVENTURE

Late in June of 1943 Lois Raney, now of Medford, Oregon, set out on one of the adventures of her lifetime. With her sister and her nine year old son, this threesome decided to ride bicycles up the state to visit relatives in Oregon. The trip was conceived of not only for the pure adventure but also to help Tony in his recovery from an accident. He had fallen from the top of a truck delivering ice in his Bay Area neighborhood, sustaining serious injuries.

But first Lois, in her mid-twenties and the mother of four, had to borrow a bike, and then learn to ride it. With little preparation, and taking not much more than a few changes of underwear, the three were dropped off out of the urban area, got on their bikes and started peddling. They cut across to the east, hit Highway 99, and headed north through the scorching Sacramento Valley.

In this day when a bicyclist would likely spend hundreds of dollars on the "proper" equipment and months in training before undertaking such a trip, their casual, can-do attitude seems amazing. The trio rode fat tired, one speed bikes and carried their few items (which did not include water) in baskets attached to the handlebars. They ate bologna sandwiches. Their severe sunburns were soothed by a concoction created by a Williams druggist.

To this day, the trip remains a pleasant, warm memory. The ride wasn't so difficult. No fears of unsavory characters. Everyone was so friendly. When they rode up to a cafe or fruit stand, everyone wanted to chat and wish them well. Although frequently asked, they never accepted a ride.

Everything went without a hitch until Lois got a flat near Dunsmuir. It was the July 4th weekend, and the clerk in the Western Auto store said they would have to wait several days to get a replacement tube. Unhappy to be left idle, they loaded their bikes onto a Greyhound bus and continued their trip up Highway 99.

Profile of Highway 99

Sacramento, CA to Ashland, OR

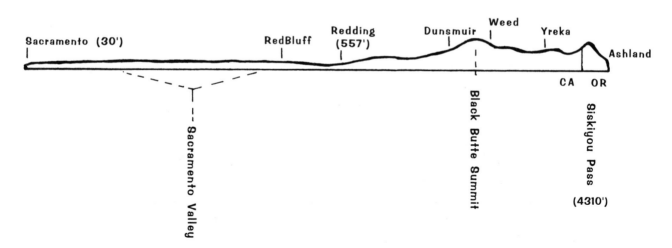

THE SACRAMENTO RIVER CANYON

The biggest challenge the highway engineers faced in the completion of Highway 99 in northern California was negotiating the Sacramento River Canyon, which stretches from a few miles north of Redding to Dunsmuir. Indisputably scenic and certainly a relief to the northbound motorist from the monotony and summer heat of the Sacramento Valley to the south, it nevertheless presented major problems in the form of steep, mountainous terrain, subsurface water that created massive slide potential, and the narrowness of the canyon that had to be shared with the train tracks.

These obstacles were merely inconveniences, if even that, to the Wintu Indians who first trod the path that Highway 99 eventually took, trading, hunting, and fishing for salmon along the river. By 1829 Caucasian fur trappers from the Hudson Bay Co. had arrived in the area. The canyon route was enlarged by one of the brigades (which were 50-100 people in size) into the Siskiyou Trail in 1837.

Before too long the discovery of gold swelled the population and the future highway became an official stage route, with a hefty $25 price tag for a Redding area to Yreka ticket. The local Stone brothers thought a better wagon road would be a good investment. They improved the road, built bridges and started charging a toll in 1861. But within the first few wintes of operation fifteen of their seventeen bridges washed away in a flood.

The Stone Road Co. seems to have made a poor investment, but this north-south course leading out of California's Central Valley continued to have importance. There was another route north, however. The alternate way headed northwest of Redding to Trinity Center, generally following the present Highway 3 over Scott Mountain, then cut back northeast to Yreka.

Both rival roads operated as stage routes for many years, each with their vocal supporters. The canyon route was rugged, but the Scott Mountain route was long. When the State finally had the funds and capabilities to begin constructing the State Highway System in the teens, the District Engineer out of Redding made the decision to have the Pacific Highway, later designated as Highway 99, generally follow the Sacramento River north.

The canyon had been partially tamed by the railroad that was built through it in the 1880s. Just about every settlement, often named after this or that far-flung railway official, had its beginnings as a railroad siding. The several scenic resorts that tourists flocked to for several decades (until automobiles eventually brought about changes in vacationing styles) were built by companies affiliated with the railroad and serviced by the frequent trains. When the highway era arrived, the road had to be located where it would not interfere with the already existing tracks so the two could safely coexist.

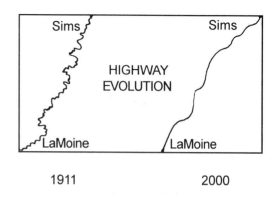

Change in the configuration of the highway north of Redding as it goes up the Sacramento River canyon.

Arrive the highway did, in the relentless march of progress precipitated by the growing popularity of automobiles. The initial goal was to make far northern California accessible by car in all seasons. From 1914 to 1919 the pace of road construction up the canyon (for the construction generally proceeded from the south to the north) was furious. Or at least as furious as work could be given the primitive tools and techniques of the day.

Even this modest road, comparatively steep and full of curves from a modern perspective, required the movement of tremendous quantities of earth with all of the cutting and filling that needed to be done. Still, the maximum grade on this part of road that was now called a State Highway decreased to 6.7% from 20%, while the minimum radius of curves increased to sixty feet from twenty feet.

71

This first phase of construction produced two noteworthy concrete arch bridges. The one at Dunsmuir, completed in 1916 incredibly, eighty years later, still carries one half of Interstate 5 on its deck. The other crossed the Pit River just north of Redding. At the time (1916) the longest concrete span in California at 242 feet, it now lies submerged deep in Shasta Lake.

As elsewhere, the mid twenties brought another surge of highway improvement in the canyon, major realignment and resurfacing, more battling of slides that threatened to inundate the road or encroach on the railroad right-of-way. Many extensive masonry retaining walls, blending so harmoniously with the surroundings, were built by uncredited craftsmen.

A few portions of the road were even paved at this time, although most of the road was surfaced with six inches of gravel and then oiled. Gravel was crushed from rock excavated from some of the large road cuts.

Bridge construction went into high gear. More of the trademark concrete arches went up over Charlie Creek, Doney Creek, Pollard's Gulch, and Dog Creek, as well as other bridges less imposing but equally important. The quest for fewer curves, gentler grades, and shorter distances continued. A well-placed bridge could cut off miles of travel.

This same stretch of canyon that we traverse in less than an hour today once required an arduous, day-long journey, if it was passable at all. Before the State started work on the highway, if you left Redding in the early morning, successfully negotiated the steep grades without overheating and didn't scrape your oil pan on a big rock, you would reach Dunsmuir by nightfall. In the summer, that is. In the winter, best not to try at all. Take the train!

By the late twenties, the Division of Highways had been on the job for fifteen years. Contemporary guidebooks characterized the road up the Sacramento Canyon as gravel-surfaced, very windy but wide and well graded. Still a lengthy trip no doubt, but given the spectacular scenery and the more relaxed attitude of the day, it must have been a pleasurable drive in good weather.

By 1932 the District Engineer in Redding declared that the highway through the canyon was "complete" and would need no further attention. He couldn't guess that another major change was less than a decade away, and in fact was already in the planning stages.

This local highway landmark was known as the Deer Head Tree. The uniquely shaped oak stood on the edge of Highway 99 in the Pine Grove area for many years until it finally rotted and fell.

SHASTA DAM AND BEYOND

Construction of the immense Shasta Dam was the most prominent part of the huge Central Valley Project. The dam was designed to hold back Sacramento River water to provide more irrigation of the fertile Central Valley farmlands that fed the burgeoning population. The lower Sacramento, McCloud, and Pit Rivers were to be inundated and forever altered As a result of that scenario, Redding achieved boomtown status during the long construction period. At the same time several other smaller communities disappeared forever beneath the rising waters...

Massive man-made, multi-armed Shasta Lake changed the entire face of the land by filling up the beautiful rugged canyons, including part of the one carrying Highway 99 and the railroad through the mountains. What this meant was relocation of about twenty seven miles of track and eighteen miles of highway (figures vary) over terrain that had been purposely avoided in the past.

This was a project that required extensive planning; specifically, eight years worth. Construction began in 1938. Again, the same difficult problems had to be faced; sharing limited space with both river and railroad, the springy, unstable ground, and the necessity of moving massive amounts of dirt.

For the first time ever, highway and railroad were being constructed in the same place at the same time. Yet highway location of necessity took a backseat to the railroad. Vehicles can negotiate steeper grades and sharper curves than trains. Rail placement took precedence wherever the two conflicted.

All factors considered, there were two feasible routes as laid out by the highway engineers. One, considered to be the more "scenic," skirted the shoreline of the proposed lake. The second was more direct but with steeper grades. The second, higher route was chosen for the sake of economy.

In the narrow confines of the canyon, it was inevitable that highway and railroad would meet at some points, and as always this raised safety concerns. In this relocated stretch of road, highway and railroad cross each other five times, but there is only one conventional underpass. Three crossings occur over tunnels and the other on the new dual-purpose (cars on the top, trains on the bottom) Pit River bridge. The highway was "completed" in 1943.

Scarcely another decade would pass before even this smooth, wide road proved to be inadequate. The postwar years saw a huge increase in vehicle traffic.

Californians had good jobs, new cars, growing families, and the urge to go someplace.

More lanes of highway were desperately needed, a major undertaking in this difficult region. For the first time aerial photos were used in surveying, saving years of time. Construction was done in bits and pieces from 1954 to 1959. The new highway covered the old, or was built on a new alignment, depending on the particular location. It was in this phase of canyon route history that many of the venerable old bridges were abandoned.

The same old problems were encountered, even increased. Besides the train tracks, there were now high-tension power lines and a coaxial telephone cable sharing the narrow space. The relentlessly increasing traffic had to be dealt with while work interruptions were kept to a minimum.

Cuts, Fills, and Slides

Then there were the massive cuts that took ugly bites out of the landscape, and the voluminous fills, both absolutely necessary to make this modern highway straight and wide and lasting.

Next, inevitably, came the slides. Here was a situation that required extensive study and experimentation before the land was stabilized and the project complete.

A seldom noticed section of masonry guard rail/retaining wall built in the mid-twenties leads into the modern freeway. The end of the finely crafted wall was crudely broken off to make way for the new highway alignment up the Sacramento River Canyon.

The problems began soon after this latest phase of canyon construction was started, for the winter of 1955-56 was a year of heavy rainfall. There were numerous large slides and one slipout of a major fill right away.

A variety of expensive but essential techniques were used to deal with the abundant underground water, and the serpentine and clay soil conditions which made poor foundations for large fills and caused slides. New, innovative designs of horizontal drains were installed, cut slopes were flattened out or benched, slide bottoms were buttressed with large rocks, retaining walls were built, stabilization trenches were dug.

One troublesome spot known as the Shiloah slip had been a problem ever since the reconstruction of 1928. Here, in the 1950s several of the new techniques were put to good use. Whereas in every winter since 1928 two to three feet of material had to be added to the roadway to restore it to its normal level, since the work was completed in 1959 it has remained stable.

In extreme cases, the highway had to be moved. Near Sweetbriar, many thousands of yards of material had already been removed from a cut when a slide developed that was simply unmanageable. To compensate for this, the highway had to be moved over away from the cut and closer to the river and train tracks. To accommodate the fill dumped over the edge to hold the new roadbed, the tracks had to be moved and a new channel dug to hold the Sacramento River. So far, it's worked.

More than any other place in our travels, it seems that this portion of Highway 99 has required continual maintenance, rerouting and upgrading. In fact it was not until 1992 that the last piece of the canyon route was brought up to full freeway status.

And even yet, more change is possible. Is California's thirst unquenchable? There has been a proposal under debate since 1983 to raise the level of Shasta Dam in order to increase its water storage capacity. This is a decision that Congress would have to approve.

A less radical approach is the likely outcome, but the original $5.6 billion plan was to raise the dam 202 feet. If that were to happen, it would be déjà vu all over again; 19 miles of highway and 36 miles of railroad would need to be rerouted, and a second Pit Bridge would be submerged beneath the lake.

CHAPTER ·13·

THE YOLO CAUSEWAY AND THE TOWER BRIDGE

These two structures are located on the very last leg of our journey down 99W to the capital, between Davis and Sacramento. US99W made a west-east jog and conjoined with US40 near Davis, so these two items are not strictly "99" phenomena, but are important nevertheless.

A permanent road could not be built across the Yolo basin because it was annually flooded with overflow from the Sacramento River. According to the 1939 Federal Writer's Project guidebook, *California,*

The deeply rutted road that formerly meandered over these swampy acres was impassable in spring when the swollen Sacramento flooded it with a muddy torrent. ...Unnumbered tons of rock had to be dumped into the swamp before the engineers won their fight.

From San Francisco and other points west, the state capital was reached in a round-about way before the Yolo Causeway was built with money from the 1910 bond issue. The 3.13 mile long, twenty-one foot wide elevated wooden trestle was finished in 1916. This was the first major bridge designed and built by the State of California. It was opened with great fanfare; a parade, "causeway specials" offered by local merchants, and the wedding of a Sacramento girl and Yolo County boy to symbolize the new link between the two counties.

Predictably, the great causeway was soon outdated. It was jammed with traffic on special occasions, yet the road was too narrow for slow vehicles to be easily passed. Before long, wooden supports were replaced with concrete pillars. Two more lanes and a sidewalk were added in 1930. In the 1960's an entirely new causeway was constructed.

The causeway heads east to the Tower Bridge and straight on to the Capitol Building. The Tower Bridge across the Sacramento River replaced the M Street Bridge in the mid-thirties.

The original 1911 structure was a swing bridge built by the Sacramento Northern Electric Railroad. Cars and trains shared the deck. The M Street Bridge was an older style movable bridge, for Sacramento was a busy port. These bridges were simple to build and operate, but required a large pier right in the center of the shipping channel. They were also notoriously slow.

000 Causeway across the Yolo Basin on the State Highway

83

A photographic postcard shows the Yolo Causeway in its earliest wooden trestle form, which was completed in 1916. A few years later concrete piers replaced the wood, more lanes and a side walk were added. An entirely new structure was built in the 1960s.

It was replaced by a more sophisticated vertical lift bridge, of which very few have ever been built in California. The consensus in 1933 was that another world war was imminent and that the M Street Bridge was barely adequate for even the current traffic. So the War Department, the State of California, Sacramento County, and the Railroad all got together to plan for the construction of a new structure. Four lanes of traffic were planned for the 52' wide roadway, including train tracks running down the middle and sidewalks on either side.

The Tower Bridge was built in the same time period as the Golden Gate Bridge and with the same attention to form as well as function. Its Streamline Moderne styling was popular in the 1930s. The Tower Bridge was specifically designed to enhance the Capital skyline, as indeed it does. It serves as one anchor point of the Capitol Mall, the other being the Capitol building itself..

The Tower Bridge is the only pre-World War II vertical lift bridge still left in the state. This beautiful landmark is visible for quite a distance, seeming to announce to the approaching motorist, "You're almost there!"

HIGHWAY 99 IS DEMOTED

As we have seen, Highway 99 grew in stages from barely more than a widened path into the smooth surfaced all important backbone of our state and reached its pinnacle in the few years just after World War II. Beyond that time, our sights were necessarily set on something more modern, a new highway concept that would better serve the burgeoning, car crazy population of California; freeways.

All road construction ground to a halt during the War. But afterward, with State funds accumulated during the war years and newly acquired Federal monies, the task of repairing and improving our highways was begun again in earnest. Automobile-driving, rapidly expanding baby boomer families validated the freeway concept, an idea first conceived of in the late 1930s.

Commercialization of roadside property eventually led to excessive on and off highway movement. All of this stopping and parking and pulling out into the flow of traffic hampered the progress of through travelers on the highways, and was dangerous besides. Defined as "a highway to which abutting property has no right of access," the freeway concept gave complete control of access to the State. The State would determine the locations of on and off ramps, so important to roadside businesses, on the multi-lane, divided roadways. "Control of access" was an unpopular idea at first, even thought by some to be illegal. The presence or lack of a nearby offramp would determine the fate of an already existing readside business.

The very first piece of California freeway was dedicated December 30, 1940, a six-mile long road that connected Pasadena and Los Angeles. It wasn't long before freeways were accepted and welcomed, their practicality proven. The 1960s saw the height of freeway construction. It was the inevitable beginning of the end for two-lane highways such as 99.

By the late 1960s all of Highway 99 in northern California was either downgraded from US Highway to State level (much of 99E from Red Bluff to Marysville), given back to local governments (such as 99W south of Red Bluff), incorporated into (or more literally, underneath) Interstate 5, or simply abandoned. That left venerable old Highway 99 for the modern day explorer to rediscover and enjoy.

A TOUR DOWN THE NORTH STATE

At the Border

Entering our great state in the 1920s. Then as now, travelers pause to capture the moment in a photograph. The first highway over Siskiyou Pass from Oregon was completed in 1915.

Just around the bend was Hilt, the first town encountered in California. Like so many of the small towns we find on Highway 99, Hilt too had its beginnings as a railroad town.

Located in the valley just to the west of the highway, Hilt later became a mill town, a company town largely dismantled in 1974 when it was no longer possible to run the mill at full production with the trees harvested from the company's surrounding timberlands.

Curiously, Hilt had a bond of sorts with other small communities hundreds of miles down the highway. Since 1910 the town has been owned by Fruit Grower's Supply Company. For many years the focus of production in Hilt was sugar pine box stock used to make fruit boxes for citrus growers in southern California. Where Highway 99 passed by a short distance up the hill from the town signs were placed on both sides that read, "This is Hilt, Where 10,000 Citrus Growers of Southern California Make Their Boxes." (Caltrans)

Bailey Hill "Separation Structure"—1949

With cars and trains sharing the same basic route up the length of California, it was inevitable that the two would occasionally cross paths. This caused safety concerns as automobile traffic increased. And so what are known as separation structures to highway engineers were built as time and funds permitted.

The first railroad underpass in this location a few miles south of Hilt and north of Hornbrook was built in 1916, soon after the highway came through. It remained in service for decades. Only twenty feet wide, a large truck and a passenger vehicle could not pass through at the same time. This bottleneck in the midst of a steep grade was the scene of numerous accidents over the years.

The thirty-two foot wide structure pictured was completed in 1948 in conjunction with a major highway improvement project through this area. It's opening was celebrated by a ribbon cutting ceremony attended by Senator Randolf Collier from this district. Senator Collier was so closely associated with endeavors such as this that he became known as "The Father of Freeways," and a prideful write-up in *California Highways*, the Division of Highways in-house magazine:

The underpass is a beautiful structure, the first major improvement of its nature that southbound traffic encounters in California. The highway grades are long and sustained. Curves are flat enough so that minimum sight distance is 1,100 feet and their number has been reduced from

46 to 10. The driving surface is of a width to provide a feeling of adequacy. The acquired right of way is sufficient to allow for the addition of two more lanes when traffic demands require them.

The structure is long gone. The at-one-time amazingly wide strip of highway now lies beneath a portion of Interstate 5. (Caltrans)

Camp Lowe

This decrepit bridge spanning the Klamath River off of Highway 99 near Hornbrook led to the fishing camp of Camp Lowe. Crossing on foot would seem to be a risky proposition today, yet vehicles used to drive across to the cabins and campground on the other side.

The Klamath is a famous salmon and steelhead river. Sportsmen came to stay at Camp Lowe for a week in the fall, passing motorists stayed for a night or two, and locals drove up from Yreka or Hornbrook to swim, grab a burger in the cafe on the near side of the river, or just hang out in the summer.

Howard Brothers
❖ **CAMP LOWE** ❖
On Klamath River . . .
13 Miles North of Yreka
. . . Elevation 2100 feet
Excellent Fishing and Hunting
Modern Cabins   Camp Supplies
"DEL" HOWARD   ✦   IVON HOWARD

Shasta River Canyon

Highway 99, now called Highway 263, crosses the Klamath River and enters the winding Shasta River Canyon eight miles north of Yreka. The highway through the canyon, first built in 1914, was completely realigned in 1929. Construction of this 1920s highway required the blasting of tremendous quantities of dirt and rock and the building of five acclaimed bridges. Its completion was considered a great accomplishment.

Taken soon after the not yet paved new highway was completed in 1931, the photograph shows the new concrete girder bridge over the Klamath with the old bridge still in place. A daily rise and fall of five or six feet in the stream flow (this was pre-dam) added to the hazards and expense of constructing the bridge footings and piers. The original bridge is gone and the open railings of the 1930 bridge are now less attractive solid walls, but this piece of the old highway is essentially unchanged. The rugged canyon was avoided when Interstate 5 came through the area in 1970, leaving this stretch of Highway 99 still widely used by local traffic and mostly intact. (Caltrans)

Aerial View of the Pioneer Bridge, Shasta River Canyon

The steel cantilever Pioneer Bridge spanning the deep Shasta River canyon was the focal point of this section of Highway 99 (now called 263) completed in 1931. The bridge rises close to 267 feet above the river and the old highway bridge and was considered quite a marvel in its day. To quote from a 1932 magazine article, "Looking down from the new bridge, the conclusion arrived at is that a cat with his back arched could scarcely crawl beneath the old bridge and not strike sparks. Regarding the dimensions of the new bridge, the fact is that the State Capitol at Sacramento could be placed in perfect clearance underneath it without danger to the highest pinnacle of its dome."

The photograph clearly shows some of the differences between the 1914 highway and the 1931 highway. The first road was low on the slopes, following the river in its every twist and turn. The later,

higher version cut rashly across the canyons and through the mountains. (The road going down the slope between the old and new highways was an access road used during highway construction.) The choice in location of this bridge cut two miles off of the previous travel distance.

In August of 1931, two caravans of cars, one from nearby Yreka and one from Oregon and each containing the governor of the respective states, converged at the bridge for a formal bridge and highway dedication. This portion of highway completed an important link between the neighboring states.

The bridge is dedicated to the pioneer stage drivers who helped forge a way through this remote and rugged country. (Caltrans)

Yreka and the State of Jefferson

Examples of two types of accommodations available to north state travelers in the forties and fifties. The auto park's "Camping-Cabins-Bathing" sounds tempting, but the classier Yreka Inn (not demolished until 1976) looks especially inviting on a snowy winter night. Auto parks or camps, the forerunners of motels, proliferated everywhere along with the automobile travelers they served. Hotels catered to the less adventurous, more affluent traveler, as well as having a local clientele that came in to drink, dine, and dance.

entrance to
Yreka auto park
Yreka Calif.

Yreka Auto Park

Highway 99 was once a tree lined promenade where it passed down Main Street. It must have been a welcome sight to the weary traveler. Yreka was the largest town between Medford, Oregon and Redding, California and is flanked by the rugged Siskiyous to the north and Mt. Shasta and the steep Sacramento River Canyon to the south. A good place to stop in forbidding weather.

Yreka was also the "capital" of the short lived State of Jefferson. If you had been traveling along Highway 99 in late November of 1941, you might have been stopped at a road block by a group of deer rifle toting men and handed a proclamation declaring, "You are now entering Jefferson, the forty-ninth state of the Union."

The "state," consisting of southwestern Oregon and California from Redding north, seceded on November 27, 1941. The movement was largely an effort to publicize, ironically, the need for good roads in the region, specifically into the more remote areas so that mineral and timber resources could be exploited. The rebellion was thwarted only a few days later with the bombing of Pearl Harbor, and the ill-fated "state" remains a minor footnote in California history. (Siskiyou County Museum)

Gazelle

Residents of the little town of Gazelle in the Shasta Valley hoped a few travelers would stop for a soda and a snack when they slowed to pass through town on their way to somewhere else. One wonders if the tacky early-1960s era sign ever enticed anyone.

A vintage Holsum Bread painting adorns the side of the now defunct general store where their purchases would have been made. This store was one of nine in a very early chain called the Denny Bar Company. They carried everything from groceries to ladies hats to barbed wire.

The original brick was plastered over in the 1930s. The store was in continuous operation from 1887 until the freeway bypassed the town in 1970.

Heading Toward "The Mountain"

14,162 foot high Mt. Shasta dominates the landscape where Highway 99 cuts a swath across the ranch lands of Shasta Valley in the 1920s. The old highway through here is basically unchanged. (Caltrans)

Approaching Weed

Wooden guardrails line a curve on a pristine stretch of old highway between Edgewood and Weed. This guard rail design was authorized by the State Highway Engineer in 1924. The new contrivance was "credited with saving the lives of Mr. and Mrs. R. Avery when their machine was struck by a motor stage" in the Division of Highway's *California Highways* magazine. The article goes on further to say that "the rear of the stage, in passing, struck his car with such force that it undoubtedly would have been hurled off the grade into the river had it not been for the guard rail."

From here the highway led travelers on to Weed and thence to Mt. Shasta City. Weed's description in a 1939 guidebook was so negative as to be almost comical, but it must have made the city fathers cringe:

Weed...is a lumber town, bleak and raw looking, in a hill-rimmed hallow. From the logged-over slopes, dotted with scrubby timber and blackened stumps, the brush sweeps down to encroach on weather-beaten houses and rickety fences. Along the railroad sidings beyond the grimy business district, spread great lumber mills with vast rows of stacked pine boards. In clearings at the edge of the brush huddle desolate, unpainted company shacks, barracklike rooming houses, and company stores.

As for the town's relationship with the highway, service stations multiplied to the point that Weed was known as "gasoline alley." But try as it might the town never became a tourist center.

Snow Zone

Whether it's 1924 (when the "winter tourist's savior" in the first photo heroically attempted to keep the highway between Weed and Mt. Shasta open),

1963 (when the car in the second photo battled the blizzard), or 2000, driving in snow is slow and treacherous. Black Butte Summit between Weed and Mt. Shasta is a notorious trouble spot in the winter. But the road crews have always done their best to keep the roads open for impatient drivers. (Sisson Museum, Caltrans)

Richfield Beacon Stations

A service station at the foot of Mt. Shasta had a prime location at the intersection of the highway to Reno, NV and US99. It was built in 1930 as part of the Richfield Beacon chain that lined Highway 99 from El Centro, CA to Tacoma, WA.

Eight of these upscale filling stations were built in California, three still standing. The one in Mt. Shasta was the only California station built in the English Norman style. It operated until 1964 when the freeway bypassed the town. All of the others were built in the California Mission style, such the one in Willows that presently houses a trucking company.

Richfield's hope was to dominate both the automobile and airplane fuel businesses. The two modes of transportation were more closely linked in those early days in that airplanes generally found their way by following highways (and train tracks.) Richfield's gimmick was the 125' tall tower with a fixed beacon on top and another beacon pointing the way to the nearest airport. A neon "Richfield" embellished one side of the tower, with the town's initials on the other side. Other stand-alone beacons were erected between the stations.

The scheme was not wholly successful. The Depression set in and people had no money to spend on unnecessary driving or flying. Around the same time the FAA took over the regulation of all airport lighting. Many planned-for Beacon stations were never built.

Dunsmuir Bridge Dedication

State and county dignitaries and officials, as well as hoards of locals showed up for the dedication of the State Highway bridge over the Sacramento River at Dunsmuir in 1916. The march of progress was recognized and welcomed for what it was—the opening up of this rugged canyon country. This bridge is a part of Interstate 5. (Siskiyou County Museum)

Dunsmuir, At the Head of the Canyon

After crossing the arch bridge spanning the Sacramento River, Highway 99 went down and through the narrow town of Dunsmuir, home of "the Best Water on Earth." Like so many other towns on the highway, Dunsmuir started out as a railroad town, a major division point complete with round house, machine shops, and offices that employed over a thousand people until the cutbacks that came with the diesel era.

The California Theater is still a going business. The sign originated in San Jose. Celebrities once appeared on the stage, including Babe Ruth (Dunsmuir was a big baseball town) and movie stars who were visiting the nearby Hearst estate, Wyntoon.

The State Highway (future US99) was a welcome addition at first, another way to bring fishermen into the area. But

what was pleasant in 1916 was a nuisance by 1950. Traffic increased from approximately one vehicle every three minutes in 1921 to three vehicles every one minute, a significant portion of it heavy trucks and buses.

Disillusion with the heavy traffic descending on the town came to a head after a fatal accident involving pedestrian school children. After that tragedy, the citizens were willing to take the feared economic consequences of being cut off by a realignment of the highway in the interest of peace and safety.

Ground was broken for a seven mile piece of new highway bypassing downtown in the late 1950s. This was to be the very first portion of full Interstate freeway in this part of California. (Historic photo courtesy of Caltrans)

Castella

An abandoned gas station and market on old Highway 99 near Castella sits only a few yards from the edge of the freeway. With no ready access, its lifeblood was cut. The business hung on fitfully until recent years. Since this photo was taken the Shell sign has been "liberated."

Establishments catering to vacationers abounded at nearby Crag View, Castle Crag, Castle Rock, and Castella—every place around here seems to have a "castle" or a "crag" in its name. Suffice it to say that the beautiful, dominating spires of Castle Crags State Park, a traveler's delight even before the park was created in 1934, seem to cast a spell over the entire area.

The Crags

Spectacular views along Highway 99 such as the Castle Crags could be better enjoyed at the slower pace of travel in 1952. Better even to stay awhile, as vacationers have done since the turn of the century. A number of resorts were located nearby. Initially, trains brought the visitors. Later the hotels and resorts served the automobile crowd as well.

The businesses flourished during Prohibition, for this area was a center of a new industry, the manufacture of illegal alcohol. Between the wars, the Crag View Open-Air Dance Pavilion was a favorite destination on a warm summer night. By the fifties these establishments had closed down. The "modern" tourist stayed in a motel or maybe camped at the State Park.

Castle Crags State Park came into being partly as a result of the stock market crash of 1929. Before that, the property was owned by a series of private developers. The last had grandiose plans for building a huge resort complex high up in the Crags accessed by a cable car system from below. When the company went broke in the crash, the State acquired the parcel that became the first piece of the new park.

The Park flowered in its early years during the Depression, for at that time the Civilian Conservation Corps built the trails, roads, campsites, restrooms, and residences. Castle Crags State Park was a fortunate product of the hard times. (Caltrans)

117

Sweetbriar

A picturesque stretch of highway in the vicinity of Sweetbriar in 1936. Mt. Shasta looms impressively in the distance, the river winds below, and the pinnacles of Castle Crags peek above the ridge line; the essence of a beautiful drive through the canyon on a sunny summer day.

The highway sits on a narrow carved-out ledge supported by a masonry retaining wall. Constructing through this portion of the canyon was the cause of much consternation among highway engineers, especially in later years when the addition of more lanes became a dire necessity. Widening the road required extensive cutting and filling, all exacerbated by the unstable land in this area. Innovative measures were taken to keep the huge land slides under control.

The valley below was once the site of a successful small industry producing hybrid strawberry plants of a variety known as Sweetbriar. (Caltrans)

The Three Bridges of Gibson

At Gibson in the Sacramento Canyon north of Redding, the three basic phases of highway development are beautifully illustrated. In this location is found the simple but serviceable concrete bridge crossing a tributary to the river marked "1915," a remnant of the first wave of State Highway construction in the teens. A short distance downstream is the higher, wider, more embellished 1928 bridge from the second phase.

Stretching high above these are two massive lengths of the freeway bridge built in 1959, the third phase. Coming from out of nowhere and disappearing into the same, the freeway crosses not only the creek but the entire canyon on two elevated spans. With each realignment, the highway appeared higher up the slopes from the river it follows, was less steep and windy, the distances shorter.

Gibson itself was never much more than a railroad siding. The train tracks follow along the bank of the river only a few feet away from the highway. In the 1880s the railroad penetrated the canyon, long a barrier to efficient north-south travel. When the need for good roads for vehicular travel became imperative, the highway was built in the narrow canyon wherever it would fit. The train tracks already occupied the best locations.

Slate Creek, LaMoine

This concrete bridge crosses Slate Creek at what was once the small mill community of LaMoine and is now just a freeway interchange. This is an example of a typical creek crossing built during the mid to late 1920s highway construction phase.

This particular bridge was built in 1927 and remained in use for about thirty years. When the earliest highway was realigned and the creek crossing moved to this location, over a mile was saved from the original five and a half mile distance between this bridge and the next major crossing at Dog Creek to the south. Shortened distances was one of the goals embodied in the official highway policy of this era.

Another of the masonry retaining walls so characteristic of the era is visible where the old highway winds back up the hill. The rubble structures built by uncredited artisans are found here and there along the old 99 route.

Dog Creek Bridge

The Harlan D. Miller Bridge over Dog Creek might be considered the jewel in the crown of highway bridges built throughout the mountainous regions of Highway 99 in the 1920s. Travelers catch a quick, tantalizing glimpse of the span from Interstate 5.

Sadly, the bridge has been vandalized. But its grandeur as well as its structural soundness endures, a tribute to the State Highway Engineer for whom the bridge was named. An observation bay with parking space and pedestrian benches was built into the structure. Decorative blue ceramic tiles were set into the railings. These flourishes are some of what set it apart from the merely functional.

The bridge was completed in 1927 and retired about 1955. Today it can be traversed only on foot. The Dog Creek Bridge is eligible to be listed on the National Register of Historic Places and will not be torn down.

Charlie Creek

Only the top of another arched bridge is visible rising out of the waters of Shasta Lake. Much of an eighteen mile stretch of Highway 99 was submerged behind Shasta Dam in the early 1940s. A short piece of the old highway was left above waterline and became part of a new road skirting the shoreline.

This bridge over Charlie Creek and a similar one over Doney Creek remained in place and above the water but had their decks raised a few feet to meet the new road level. Both were built in steep canyons with rock outcroppings, ideal locations for high arch bridges.

Still Above Waterline

A gas station on a piece of Highway 99 abandoned when the construction of Shasta Dam necessitated a highway realignment, now on a shoreline road.

Secrets Revealed

Droughts aren't all bad. A low Shasta Lake in 1994 exposed two treasures that aren't frequently seen. These two bridges have been submerged for most of the last nearly sixty years, since the construction of Shasta Dam necessitated the rerouting of Highway 99.

Now a makeshift road used by fishermen in search of water to fish, the pre-1942 highway crosses Salt Creek and winds its way along the creek bed. The road and bridge are normally under water in the Salt Creek Inlet of Shasta Lake.

A small bridge across O'Brien Creek in the bottom of what should be the O'Brien Creek Inlet may have been damaged by flotsam in the lake or perhaps a boat. This bridge style, found also in other spots along the highway, is made of concrete but appears to be modeled after a wooden bridge.

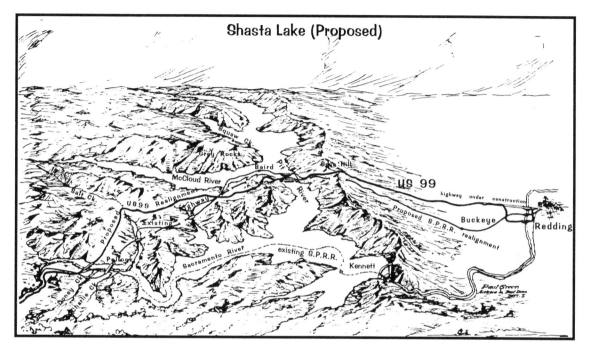

A relief sketch map from a 1935 issue of *California Highways and Public Works* shows just how several miles of Highway 99 and Southern Pacific Railroad would need to be relocated before the lake could fill following Shasta Dam's construction. Many years of careful planning went into this realignment. (Map by Paul Green and Bart Dunn of Dist. II)

Pit River Bridge

This was still a ferry crossing when the road through here was first designated as a State Highway. The Pit River Inn sits near the south approach to the long concrete arch that was built over the river a couple of years later, in 1916. Another beautiful bridge in a beautiful setting; it was built to last but not destined to.

Around 1933 the Division of Highways started planning for the eventual relocation of eighteen miles of Highway 99 to replace that which would be inundated by the waters behind the proposed Shasta Dam. Location of the bridge over what would become the Pit arm of the lake was critical, for its location would help determine the new alignment of the highway on the other side. A site just downstream from the first bridge was chosen.

The new bridge had to be very high and very long to cross what would be a lake rather than a river. It was the largest single construction item resulting from the highway relocation.

The photograph shows the 3200' long bridge under construction about 1940, safety net in place. The tallest of the piers is 358' tall and 90' by 95' at the base. Metal tubing embedded in the piers circulated river water for cooling, a practice first developed for use in dam construction. The unique design called for automobile traffic to be carried on the top deck with train tracks down below, for the railroad had to be relocated as well. The old Pit crossing is dwarfed in comparison.

The new roadway was completed on schedule but not the connecting bridge. The project would likely have been drawn out for several more years had it not been for World War II. Good open roads were considered a must for national defense. In order that work on the bridge could continue no matter what the weather, a giant $20,000 tarp was suspended over the structure. The new dual-purpose bridge was opened in the spring of 1942, and the old concrete span was

slowly inundated by the rising waters. (Shasta Historical Society)

"The Miracle Mile"

The 99 Motel is only one of many along the strip in north Redding commonly called the "Miracle Mile." One might wonder how this stretch of road acquired such a name.

In fact, this name is a holdover from fifty years ago. As it turns out, many growing cities had Miracle Miles of their own. They are examples of just one way that automobiles influenced the changing characters of cities.

Miracle Miles are a reflection of the shifting of businesses from the downtown area and out to the edge of town. Before WWII the "approach strip" on the way into town held auto courts (the motorist's prefered alternative to the downtown hotel), gas stations, produce stands.

After the War there was sudden prosperity: new cars, plenty of gas, and money to spend. Soon supermarkets, auto dealers, hardware stores were built along the approach. All were set back from the street, easily accessible by car, and there was plenty of room to park. After the long hard years of Depression and war, the quick transformation into a bustling shopping area seemed like an economic miracle.

Diestelhorst Bridge

Before 1914 the north or southbound traveler crossed the Sacramento River at Redding by ferry. The City of Redding was instrumental in financing and locating this highway bridge, as the State's planned route would direct highway traffic away from the town and across another bridge.

Initially known as the Reid's Ferry Bridge, the Diestelhorst Bridge was the first reinforced concrete bridge to span the Sacramento River. An auto camp with gas station and open-air dance pavilion was located on the south side of the bridge.

The Redding landmark is still in use today, although Highway 99 was moved a short distance to the east when a new, wider bridge was completed in 1936. Both the new and the old bridge suffered flood damage in 1940, keeping the two sides of town isolated from each other for a time.

This bridge and the wide expanse of river below it known as Lake Redding were important to the fabric of the town's daily life, especially in the hot summer. As traffic bound from other parts of the state whizzed by, daredevils dove from the bridge to the thrill of their friends down below. The "lake" was a gathering spot for all of the town, young and old alike, on a summer's evening. The swimming area was originally at the south side of the bridge but a new one was built on the north side by WPA labor in the 1930s.

Another Way to Get There

Redding's fine example of an old Greyhound bus terminal is still an active place. It reminds us that you have never had to actually own a car to take to the highways.

Bus travel is in some ways a carry over from the stage coach days of old. This mode of commercial passenger travel fell into disfavor when the railroads came in, but slowly regained popularity when the "coaches" were motorized and the limits of train travel were realized. Early buses were called "auto stages".

The earliest "buses" were not vehicles that had been designed especially for their task. They were modifications of cars that were already being manufactured, such as Hupmobiles and Packards. By the time Greyhound Lines Inc. was formed in 1930 this was no longer the case. Powerful, sturdy built-to-order Mack buses plied the often bumpy roads to provide affordable Depression-era transportation for the masses.

Many small bus lines had come and gone in the early days of the highway era, such as the Pickwick Lines in this part of the state. But Greyhound was the first company to have a nation-wide network. Hundreds of local bus companies were brought under the Greyhound wing. Many attractive Art Deco style Greyhound terminals were built in larger towns and cities throughout the 1930s to 1940s.

139

Redding's Christmas Tree

North state motorists heading out for the holidays were greeted for many years by a giant Christmas tree coming right out of a manhole in the middle of an intersection as they slowed to pass through Redding on Market St. (Highway 99). At another time of the year, on afternoons in the hot valley summers, Market St. was where locals parked their cars to cool off in the shade of downtown buildings.

Redding is located right at the head of the Sacramento Valley, the end of the straight, flat highway and the beginning of the climb up through the Sacramento River canyon. It became something of a boom town during the late 1930s and early '40s when Shasta Dam was being built and US99 and the train tracks were being relocated. However, "construction workers" were generally viewed as unruly types, not suitable for your daughter or sister to go out with. (Shasta Historical Society)

Cottonwood to Red Bluff

Leaving Redding, the old highway followed the train tracks to Anderson, described in a 1930s guidebook as "dingy." In the late '40s fully one half of the Highway 99 businesses, those on the west side of the road, were leveled when the highway was widened to four lanes.

Then on to Cottonwood, another typical, small agricultural town that, like all the others, tried to squeeze a few pennies out of passing highway motorists. Cottonwood's claim to fame was "The Bee Capital of the West." The Montgomery Ward catalog shipped bees from Cottonwood all over the country.

The trip down US99 from Cottonwood to Red Bluff in 1940 was a pleasant drive through grassy undulating hills dotted with Valley Oaks. Today the road is straighter and wider and no longer negotiates the thirteen curves of Cottonwood Hill, but the scenery is much the same; a slice of old California. A piece of old highway crossing a bridge stamped "1915" is isolated between the north and southbound lanes of Interstate 5.

On reaching Red Bluff (important in pre-highway days for being the furthest point upriver that the Sacramento could be navigated) the motorist had to make a choice between two rival alternate routes, 99 East and 99 West. The East Side Highway Association tried to persuade them to "turn left at Red Bluff" by posting billboards from Oregon on down, and painting a huge left-pointing arrow on a building in Red Bluff. But 99W seems to have been the preferred route to the State Capital. (Historic photo courtesy of Caltrans)

Cottonwood, Long Bridge Coming Down

It's hard not to notice this handsome old US99 bridge right alongside I-5 at the crossing of Cottonwood Creek. Besides its good looks and length (nearly a third of a mile) this structure's claim to fame is the fact that it rests in two separate counties, Tehama on the south side and Shasta to the north. It was built in 1930 and the governor of California officiated at the dedication. Sadly, this bridge is scheduled to be torn down soon. Let's hope the authorities change their minds about replacing this still servicable landmark.

Chico, "The Rose City of Butte County"

A 1959 Chico winter street scene, no roses blooming yet, on broad Esplanade Ave. which once was Highway 99. Chico was the biggest and by far most sophisticated town along 99E, a college town bisecting a string of small agricultural communities.(Caltrans)

For many decades passing travelers and locals alike sought the shade of the gargantuan Hooker Oak for picnics. Located in Chico's Bidwell Park, it was judged to be one of if not the largest oak in the world, with a large enough canopy to provide shade for 9,000 people on a hot summer's day. (At two square feet per person, no stretching out allowed.) It fell a victim to old age and a windstorm in 1977.

A Chico pub still bore the name of the old highway on our first trip through town, but it has since been renamed.

Straight and Clean

A clean line of single-slab concrete cuts a swath through the blooming fruit orchards of the Sacramento Valley in the early 20th Century. Summer dust and winter mud were no longer a concern. With plentiful water from the irrigation projects orchard acreage expanded. Good roads made it easy to transport the produce to market.(Caltrans)

Rice, Rice and More Rice

Grain elevators are a common feature of the valley skyline along Highway 99, both East and West. They loom in the windshield view ahead; their bulk fills the rearview mirror; their symmetrical shapes rise from the flat earth with a certain purpose.

Rice is the grain most frequently processed in these plants, the product of the many acres of shimmering green and watery fields that challenge the intense summer heat and enhance the highway motorist's vista.

What's so appealing to the human eye also attracts waterfowl to a feast, as well it should; California's rice belt is smack in the heart of the Pacific Flyway for migrating waterfowl. Rice farmers have come up with clever devices to scare away the birds. On the other hand, rice is grown especially for the birds in some wildlife areas.

Early in the 20th century a Japanese cook is purported to have planted thirty acres of rice with seed from his native country. It was a rousing success and before long the government set up the Biggs Field Rice Experimental Station.

With abundant water tapped from nearby rivers, an agreeable climate, fertile soil, and the government footing the bill to figure out the most efficient methods for growing the crop, this area found itself producing 80% of California's rice crop. Rice growing is one of the most mechanized agricultural operations in the State.

151

Durham, And Beyond

This view of the Durham area in 1944 shows how closely Highway 99 often followed the train tracks. Trains were the first means of transporting the area's produce, but by mid-century trucks and good highways for them to drive on were equally (or more) important.

Much of this part of the Sacramento Valley was developed in the early 1900s by the founding of "colonies." These were large tracts of land subdivided by farseeing developers into smaller parcels that aspiring farmers could afford. Even the State got onto the act in the Durham area where one colony in 1918 was founded especially for WWI war veterans. Advertising was done all over the country, attracting many easterners to California. Often the best adapted local crops were determined by government experimental stations; later the government funded irrigation projects. All was in place for the successful cultivation of the Sacramento Valley.

And so myriad little farming towns sprouted along train tracks and highways. When the highway gained importance, the little towns then sprouted gas stations and auto courts.

To a motorist traveling down 99E the towns must have seemed interchangeable. Yet each tried to forge an identity of its own. Biggs was "The Mill City, In the Heart of the Rice Belt." Gridley has lately become "The Kiwi Capital of the World," which shows how more exotic crops are being grown as public taste widens. Yuba City was "The Peach Bowl of the World." Wheatland was known as the largest producer of hops in the world. As such it was also the site of California's first field worker's strike in 1913. Lincoln was the odd town out, known for its dirt (clay) rather than what can be grown in it.

The East Side Highway, future US99E, wasn't fully paved until 1922. The highway was dedicated in June of that year in Red Bluff, where 99E splits from

99W. A writeup in *Motorland* brags about the "141 miles of unbroken concrete" that "passes through eighteen cities and towns and five counties". (Caltrans)

Twin Cities in a "Peach Bowl"

As Highway 99 approaches the two riverine cities of Yuba City and Marysville the traveler can't help but notice the surprising humps of nearby Sutter Buttes rising out of the fields and orchards to the west. These eroded volcanic craters have been dubbed "the world's smallest mountain range."

But of more concern to local residents have been the Feather and Yuba rivers which converge here, and their penchant for flooding. The two towns flourished in the Gold Rush days yet the mining was nearly their undoing. Unchecked hydraulic mining upriver caused massive flood debris to nearly bury the towns, especially Marysville. The Drainage Act of 1880 turned the tide, so to speak, away from mining and toward agriculture.

The resulting watershed studies lead to the irrigation projects of the early 20th century that would turn this area into the mid-century "Peach Bowl." The Cling Peach was developed locally.

These days the area is more of a Prune Dish, Rice Bowl or Tomato Platter. The largest prune packing plant in the world is Sunsweet Growers Inc. in Yuba City.

154

155

Lincoln's Clay

The little town of Lincoln found it's niche 125 years ago and has never strayed. Gladding, McBean and Company **is** Lincoln. That and the World War II military training airport built nearby in 1942.

Row upon row of red clay pipe is stacked in the yards of the expansive manufacturing plant along old Highway 99. Multi-hued piles of clay are protected from the weather under open-sided sheds. The workers, many of them long term loyal employees, practice their craft in the cavernous buildings with tall chimneys.

And craftsmen they are, for sewer pipes are only the most basic of the items manufactured here, if the most numerous. This company manufactures everything from the decorative terracotta used to adorn buildings to bas-relief murals to huge round state seals.

The local clay was discovered by coal miners in 1874. The quality and quantity of the deposit is enough that Lincoln will likely be famous for its clay works well into its third century of operation.

Roseville

The Tower Theater in Roseville no longer shows movies but the locals want it to stay, an icon to the simpler pleasures of yore. The theater sits on a main downtown street that was at one time the US99 (and US40) alignment. Roseville is a Sacramento suburb that has kept a small town atmosphere.

Roseville has always been a transportation town although the highways came later. The sounds of churning engines, creaking wheels and shrill whistles are still pervasive, but it's likely the locals barely notice it.

The rail yards that were moved here in 1906 are still active. Perhaps more famous was the Pacific Fruit Express ice plant from the 1920s. Here is where northern California's precious and perishable bounty was packed into boxcars full of ice and sent out across the nation.

At Roseville Highway 99 joined with Highway 40 for an east-west jog. The two US highways were conjoined through the state capital and split again near Davis, where US40 headed for San Francisco and 99W turned north toward the Oregon border.

159

Retro North Sacramento

We found Iceland in the sprawling city outskirts of North Sacramento. Aunt and niece swung out of the double wooden doors grinning with pleasure after a session. What a surprise that not all ice skating rinks are in malls, that today's urban youth can have the same ice skating experience that we had back in the 1950s. The building is studded with colored tiles and clear glass blocks.

How convenient that two icy spots are right next door to each other. According to a worker at the American Ice Co., the "ice" sign was brought over from the 1937 Paris World's Fair and was one of the first neon signs in Sacramento.

161

99W - Orchards and Palms

Heading south from Red Bluff, it's a pretty drive down 99 in the Corning/Orland area. The highway is faced with orchards, groves, and residences such as this palm-lined orchard estate near Richfield. Much of this area was divided into small parcels around the turn of the century and sold to prospective orchardists, ten acres being sufficient acreage to make a living if fruit was the crop. Olives and oranges are the major fruits grown.

Olive City

The gnarled trunk of an olive tree is an apt symbol of the venerable, dependable olive industry so closely associated with the Corning ("Olive City") area. All over town and along the road going north or south the Highway 99 traveler could purchase olives prepared an infinite variety of ways. At one time there were seven olive processing plants in town.

Very early on, Corning residents recognized the importance of the highway traveler to the local economy. The state's very first Municipal Auto Camp was built amongst olive and orange trees in Corning in 1900. For 50 cents for the first day and 25 cents a day thereafter, the auto camper was provided with a picnic table, electricity, stoves, restrooms, and cement wash tubs. The camp is now a shady city park.

As time went on, more auto camps and courts were built in tree-shaded spots along the highway; Camp Olive, the Orchard Inn and Motel; and stayed popular up through the fifties.

Between Corning and Orland

The small metal skeleton of an old gas station stood forlorn along old Highway 99 until the late 1990s, a humble prelude to the large present-day truck stop a short distance up the road. Now all that remains is the cement slab it sat on.

Prefabricated gas stations such as this one first came on the scene in the teens and were common in the 1920s. They were small (around 15'x 15' depending on the manufacturer), inexpensive (about $2200) and relatively easy to bolt together, or even take apart and relocate. With that in mind, it's a wonder the collectors held off so long on this one.

In the evolution of the gas station, this metal prefab was at the cave man stage but well past the apes. The hose-and-funnel setup of 1905 was a curbside pump with underground tank by 1910. Then the flammable "filling station" (as they came to be called) was moved to a safer offstreet drive-in "shed," still in the central business district. By the 1920s, neighborhoods had their own "house" style filling stations, some of them increasingly elaborate in design.

The Corning station was a "house with canopy" style. The earliest cars were open and were not usually driven in inclement weather. By the 1920s that was no longer the case. Station attendants appreciated the weather protection that the canopy gave.

166

Fruit Stands, Snake Pits, and Glassblowers

For some reason, the straight swath of Highway 99 going through the Corning and Orland area was lined with places for the automobile traveler to stop, get something to eat or drink, even be entertained. On reaching this part of the state, perhaps it was just time to take a break, to be relieved from the monotony of driving and the flat expanse of the valley.

Whatever the reasons, this stretch of highway was dotted with fruit stands built mainly to cater to the highway traveler, few of which survived the opening of Intestate 5 except in the form of tumble-down remains. These businesses, sometimes situated on the road in front of the owner's farm, sold olives of all types, oranges and other fresh local produce, local specialties such as "French fried almonds" or turkey sandwiches (there was once a turkey industry in the area), and of course ice cold (very important on a 100 degree-plus summer day) orange juice and apple cider. Often these treats were enjoyed at a picnic table placed under a shady arbor. The Olive Mart ("Specializing in Turkey Sandwiches") was located "on the curve" in Corning and also sold such treats as fried grasshoppers, dried worms, and rattlesnake and turtle meat. (Corning Museum.)

Other businesses were more novel. Glassblowers would produce (in fact, still will) a glass figure before your eyes; maybe a gift item for the aunt you were on the way to visit, along with that jar of olives for your uncle.

The second photograph (from 1995) shows the disheveled remains of what was known as "The Snake Pit." All that is left of the building today is its shell; the wood siding and upper story have all been removed.

The Snake Pit was a sort of local side show featuring exotic snakes and reptiles the likes of which one would more likely expect to see along a desert highway. The creatures were occasionally transported to other places to appear in shows and movies; the trucks are still parked behind the building. Local

hearsay has it that, on learning of the proposed freeway construction, the reptiles' owner petitioned for an offramp to access his place of business. Figuring his business was doomed when it was not forthcoming, (although one might think, freeway or not, the era of that type of entertainment was passing), the story is that he picked up an ax and forthwith dispatched his charges to the hereafter. Hmmmm.

170

Welcome to Our Town

The welcoming arch or sign was a highway fashion that first appeared soon after the turn of the century but really flourished in the twenties and thirties. The very first arches were intended for the train riding public and were so oriented to be seen from the depot.

Soon however, highways became an increasingly important means of bringing non-locals into the area. In fact a better one, for automobile travelers can move about, and stop at will. So welcoming arches and signs, usually illuminated, began to appear over the highways at the entrances to many towns. The idea was to distinguish this little town in some way from the similar one a few miles back, to give the visitors a friendly welcome and hopefully entice them to stay awhile and spend a little money.

The arches were a tangible expression of civic pride. Along with the town's name some type of slogan was often included such as "Gateway to the Sierras" or "Home of the Peach." In later years the arches often fell into disrepair and disfavor. Arches were "old fashioned." Their low heights and narrow widths impeded traffic. Highway officials didn't like them.

Highway 99 north of Sacramento had its share of welcoming arches and signs. The arched "Yreka" sign was hung over the intersection of Main (Highway 99) and Miner Streets in 1917. It stayed there for about fifty years, languished for several more years in the city yard, and was happily resurrected in 1976. It no longer spans the highway but welcomes visitors at the central Yreka interchange.

Weed also has its arch, although not the original structure. The first arch (in the same location as the present arch) was built of concrete over steel rails. It was torn down in 1963 due to its weakening. One questions the validity of this assessment since it took three weeks to dismantle the old arch. After a hard fought effort to bring the community together behind the project, a new steel "Weed Arch" was erected in 1990.

A few miles south the highway was spanned by a simple "Mt. Shasta City" sign. This welcoming sign was erected when the town effected a name change. Formerly called Sisson, the new name was chosen as more marketable, more readily identifiable with the locality.

Down in the valley, Corning also had a sign bridging the highway. It was erected in 1907, and declared Corning to be "The Clean Town," a reference to the fact that it was a "dry" town at that time. During Prohibition the whole country was "dry" so that slogan lost its significance. In 1924 Corning became "The Olive Town," an identity that still rings true, although the sign is long gone.

Orland's arch at the north side of town is a beautifully preserved stuccoed structure built in 1926. It's 43 foot height saved it from the fate of other arches which were demolished in the wake of larger trucks carrying taller loads. An

173

174

identical arch planned for the south side of town never materialized. Constructing the first one seems to have drained the town of its funds and its goodwill.

The Williams arch was oriented toward the train station but clearly visible from the Highway 99 a block away. The arch is of steel supported by masonry pillars (later faced with brick.) It was erected in 1917, refurbished in 1985, and still stands.

Cool Places

In years gone by this decaying establishment near Artois doubtlessly dispensed many a cold brew to parched-throated highway travelers.

To others, the scenery a few miles down Highway 99 in the vicinity of Blue Gum Road was more refreshing. This part of the old highway was (and is) a delightful shady oasis in the midst of the flat valley.

Eucalyptus was introduced from Australia in 1853. It never panned out as a lumber-producing tree as had been envisioned. Eucalyptus has been used for firewood, for windbreaks, and to drain marshes, not to mention to provide shade, and to fill the air with its wonderful fragrance. To many people long rows or whole forests of the deliciously pungent trees are part of the California experience.

Giant Orange

The remains of a "Giant Orange" on the south edge of Williams look a bit forlorn and not very giant. Giant Oranges, Mammoth Oranges, Big Oranges, and other orange stuccoed orbs were a familiar sight along Highway 99, in other parts of California, and Florida. This one, not a part of the original chain, was erected in the thirties by the owners of a nearby motel. Another (still open) Orange is located on piece of former Highway 99 near Redding at Pine Grove, this one built as a part of the original franchise.

The first such roadside refreshment stand was opened in Tracy, CA by Frank Pohl in 1926. He franchised the Giant Orange name and opened several other restaurants up and down the state, the majority situated on 99 south of Sacramento. They dispensed orange juice and other citrus based specialties along with burgers and hot dogs, and even draft beer. The oranges were designed to be movable and as such were sometimes moved to new locations when sold or a highway was moved.

This roadside genre emerged between the Wars, when there were no restrictions on garish designs or outlandish signs; not beautiful, but nonetheless humorous relief from sometimes monotonous road travel. This era spawned many animal or object shaped buildings in the form of donuts, hot dogs, milk bottles, etc., in other localities, the precursors of the giant neon "golden arches" that were soon to follow.

Motels

Brightly lit neon motel signs from the forties and fifties were a welcome sight to late night motorists. Motels were a fairly recent development when these establishments were built: more casual than a hotel, more comfortable than an auto court. Motel chains were not invented yet, so each concern had its very own name and distinctive neon sign to set it apart from all the rest. Once on the main highway but now off the beaten track, some motels survive by serving the budget minded traveler, while others have been turned into apartments.

181

A glint of clean white concrete caught the corner of my eye. And there on a straight stretch of 99 near Zamora was a "C Block" poking up it's head on the strip of ground between the old highway and the railroad tracks. How had this monument survived so unscathed for three quarters of a century or more?

C Blocks were placed along California's state highways (hence the "C") from 1914 until 1934. Highway 99 (or Pacific Highway as it was then called) was of course initially a California State Highway. After the 1916 Federal Aid Road Act it became a State Highway built partially with federal aid, and in 1926 it officially became US99.

The purpose of the blocks was to provide permanent survey monuments for accurate deliniation of the highway right-of-way from private porperty. We have found them scattered here and there along the older Highway 99 alignments. Further north the "C"s are often filled with moss.

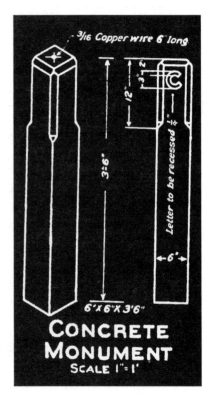

CONCRETE
MONUMENT
SCALE 1"=1'

Keep your eyes peeled! After a first spotting the next ones come easier, and you begin to wonder why you never noticed them before.

The diagram is from a 1927 Highway Commission blueprint.

Crossing Cache Creek

Highway and railroad cross the same creek side-by-side near the town of Yolo on the old 99 route. Without getting out for a look, the motorist has no idea that a pretty concrete arch lies beneath the deck of the highway bridge.

Yolo is described as *an old fashioned town with rutted streets and old houses, picket fences, and many walnut trees* in a 1939 guidebook. It doesn't appear to have changed much.

The very earliest experiments in irrigation in this area were done with water diverted from Cache Creek.

Woodland

Prudent, cautious and hard-headed businessmen predict that Woodland will soon become known as one of the wealthiest and most beautiful of the home towns in California. It is located on Route 99, the government road, and the surrounding country is known far and wide for its excellently paved highways. You will always find a welcome in Woodland.

So said the Yolo County Board of Trade in the 1931 *Tourist Town Guide of the Pacific Highway.* In more recent times, the car dealer made the right choice by not replacing the classic neon signs. In the background, old downtown Woodland fortunately is still alive.

Davis, next town along the line, is known for Jerome Davis' farm (now UC Davis) and is populated with thousands of bicycles.

Entering the Capital

California's capital arose along the edge of the river that carried Gold Rush prospectors landing in San Francisco inland closer to the gold fields. The capitol building itself sits not far from the Sacramento River's banks. The Tower Bridge crosses the river that US99 has generally followed on its way down the valley. The structure provides a grand gateway into the city.

Standing on the capitol building steps, the 160' tall towers have been a dominant figure in the foreground of the western sunset since the bridge's Dec. 15, 1935 dedication.   Governor Mirriam was the first to cross the bridge on that day. The ribbon broken by his radiator signaled the bridge's official opening. A blaring multitide of sirens and car and ship horns followed, as well as the furious flapping of wings when 1000 pigeons were released to mark the occasion.

The Tower Bridge was built to replace the M Street Bridge. It originally carried the tracks of the Sacramento Northern Electric Railroad as well as four lanes of traffic.

PART

3

Appendix: Following the 99 Trail

Highway 99 was almost always the main street going through the heart of the towns on our route; hence its reputation as "the Main Street of California."

But between the towns, keep in mind that except in the Central Valley, Highway 99 survives mostly in unidentified fragments crisscrossed by the freeway, and for this reason is often difficult to follow. Much of what can't be found was buried beneath the thick pavement of the new Interstate. Surely some pieces of the old road have been overlooked in this appendix; corrections and additions are welcomed.

While discovering some or all of these severed bits of the old highway, the pieces of the puzzle begin to fit together. We see how the now antiquated but venerable old road climbed up and wound around and crossed over the land in its unfailing march up and down the state. Acting as roadside archeologists by coupling the artifacts left behind with a little imagination, it's fun to conjure a mental image of the bygone era as we drive along.

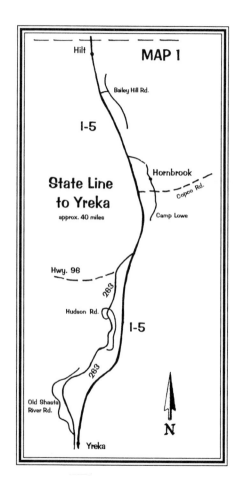

MAP 1

Hilt

Bailey Hill Rd.

I-5

**State Line
to Yreka**

approx. 40 miles

Hornbrook

Copco Rd.

Camp Lowe

Hwy. 96

263

Hudson Rd.

I-5

263

Old Shasta
River Rd.

Yreka

N

Oregon Border to Yreka: Map 1

Highway 99 is buried beneath the freeway at the state line. The early, pre-99 highway of the teens and twenties can be accessed at the **Hilt** turnoff. From the east side of the freeway, take Jefferson Rd. north back toward Oregon—this is the area shown on p. 89.

The first piece of intact Highway 99 is reached at Bailey Hill Rd. (p.91) Here on the east side of the freeway heading south from the offramp is a fragment of the old road that soon crosses our first example of early concrete highway bridge (the same style as on p. 130). Return to the freeway.

The next piece of 99 turns up at the **Hornbrook** Highway exit and takes us south through the small town on Hornbrook Road. Cross Copco Road and continue until reaching our first abrupt end at the edge of the freeway, just past Camp Lowe (p.93) Backtrack to Copco Road and get back on the freeway.

Take the Highway 96, Klamath River Highway exit, the next exposed piece of 99. At the 96/263 intersection, follow 263 (pp.95, 97)) into **Yreka** (See Chapter 9). Through here note the five bridges built in the twenties, the masonry guard rails/retaining walls, and the original 1914 highway down by the river.

Hudson Road accesses a piece of the 1914 highway, taking us directly underneath one of the concrete arch bridges, and ending below the Pioneer Bridge (p.97). Farther along, Old Shasta River Road is also a piece of the earliest highway, providing an excellent view of the arch bridge over Dry Gulch.

Yreka to Mt. Shasta: Map 2

Main Street right through **Yreka** is the old highway. (pp.99,101)) The refurbished arched "Yreka" sign (p. 173) is located at the central Yreka interchange.

At Oberlin Rd., go under the freeway and continue south on Fairlane until reaching another "abrupt end." You will cross another small bridge in very poor condition in the same "imitation wood" style as the one we saw at Bailey Hill. Backtrack to Walters Lane, go over the top to the west side of the freeway, and continue south on Easy St.

At Shamrock Rd. go back under the freeway to reach another piece of old highway. You can travel either north or south for a short distance. Heading south takes you past the defunct Shamrock Restaurant (a perfect example of a business whose lifeblood was cut off by the Interstate) where the old highway ends. The old route reappears on the other side of the freeway.

Back on Easy St.and heading south, this road is eventually identified as "Old Highway 99." It continues for a number of miles taking us through **Gazelle** (pp.102,103) and across the Shasta Valley (p.105).

Take the turn for **Edgewood** which goes under the freeway again; turn south on Edgewood Rd. (p. 107) and cross a well-preserved small concrete bridge. In this vicinity was located the 99 Ranch, which catered to locals and travelers alike with its gas station, garage, dance hall, and saloon. Nothing remains. Look for the "C Block" (see p.182) high on a cut bank before you get to Weed.

At **Weed**, go south on Weed Blvd. The Weed arch (not the original one, see p. 144) is located at the original Highways 99 and 97 intersection. 97 is billed as the start of the Alaska Highway, thus the totem pole in the grocery store parking lot.

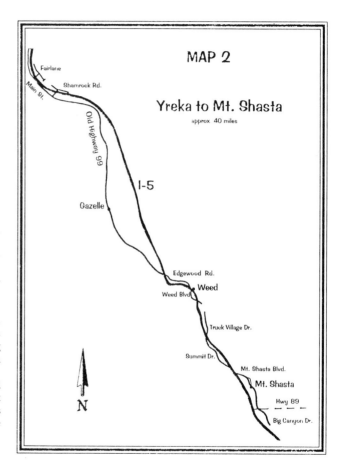

191

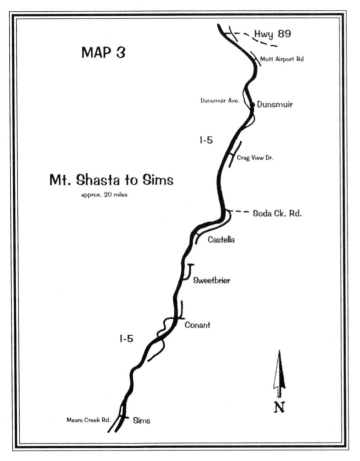

MAP 3

Hwy 89

Mott Airport Rd

Dunsmuir Ave.　Dunsmuir

I-5

Crag View Dr.

Mt. Shasta to Sims

approx. 20 miles

Soda Ck. Rd.

Castella

Sweetbrier

Conant

I-5

N

Mears Creek Rd.　Sims

Continue through town, then turn left on Shastina Dr. This piece of old highway ends at the new South Weed conglomerate of fast foods and filling stations, a modern traveler's dream.

Back on the freeway, take the **Truck Village** exit right at the foot of Black Butte (pp.108,109.) This cinder cone was the ready source of much of the gravel used in highway construction in this part of the state. Truck Village Dr., on the east side of the freeway, is a piece of the old highway winding a mile or two back toward Weed.

Return the way you came, but instead of getting back on the freeway, go over to the west side and continue south on Summit Dr. Much of the old highway is buried through here, but one of its old curves snakes over to the west side near where Summit Dr. passes the Shasta Abbey (which was a motel in the early days) then loops back under the freeway again. Also in this area was a railroad spur line where Black Butte gravel was loaded for transporting to highway construction sights. Unlucky was the traffic stopped at the crossing for what seemed like an interminable time while the train was loaded.

To pick up the 99 trail again, return to the freeway at Abram's Lake, then take the first **Mt. Shasta** exit to Mt. Shasta Blvd. which was Highway 99 going through town. A nice example of the typical rock retaining walls we saw north of Yreka and will see more of below

Dunsmuir lines a curve soon after the freeway exit. Continue through the town.

The very earliest highway alignment followed Chestnut St., which still retains the original concrete pavement, rather than Mt. Shasta Blvd. Another little piece of original concrete is left just south of the Humane Society near the north entrance to town.

After passing the old Richfield Beacon gas station (p.111) at the Highway 89/99 intersection at the south end of town, the old highway can be followed on Big Canyon Dr. for a short distance from the south side of Highway 89 until it is abruptly cut off by the freeway. Return to Interstate 5 via Highway 89.

Mt. Shasta to Sims: Map 3

Heading south again, Highway 99 next reappears at Mott Rd. From the east side of the freeway, going either right or left on Mott Airport Rd. (p.50) puts us back on the old highway. **Mott** was a thriving railroad/ mill town at the turn of the century: nothing remains except the name.

Returning to the west side of the freeway, turn south. Soon Mott Rd. turns into Dunsmuir Ave., and we're back on Highway 99. We pass Shasta Springs on our right. This was one of the spectacular resorts that had its beginnings during the railroad era. It continued to serve vacationers and bottle its prize-winning mineral water through the first half of the twentieth century. Since 1950 it has been owned by the St. Germain Foundation, one of the Mt. Shasta-oriented religious groups. A short way past the gated entrance, almost hidden in the young trees is the original narrow stone and iron arched entryway.

Staying on **Dunsmuir** Avenue, near the next freeway onramp is a pretty little park with a short trail down to Hedge Creek Falls. The Falls were almost buried by the I-5 construction in the late sixties but were saved by local outcry.

Continuing south, it is easy to imagine driving down this piece of shady, motel-lined Highway 99 forty years ago, trying to decide which place to stay. Dunsmuir Avenue veers off of the old 99 route to cross the Sacramento River, then returns as it goes through Dunsmuir (pp. 113, 114). Look to your left when crossing the river to note southbound Interstate 5 crossing on the concrete arch built in 1916. (p.112)

Soon after going through town on the old highway, we are forced onto the freeway, and the old highway disappears.

From here on out through the canyon, it's mostly a matter of taking each freeway exit and seeing where it takes us, then returning to the freeway. Here more than anywhere the old highway has been chopped up and covered up to the extent that it takes some detective work to follow the trail; but that's where the fun lies.

The first exit past Dunsmuir is **Crag View** Dr., another piece of the old highway that takes us a short distance either north or south. We cross an old cement highway bridge with pipe railings if we turn north toward Dunsmuir. The Railroad Park Motel is worth checking out for its numerous caboose "motel rooms" and spectacular Crag view. Then, back to the freeway.

Take the next exit, **Soda Creek** Rd., go under the freeway and turn south on the old highway, now

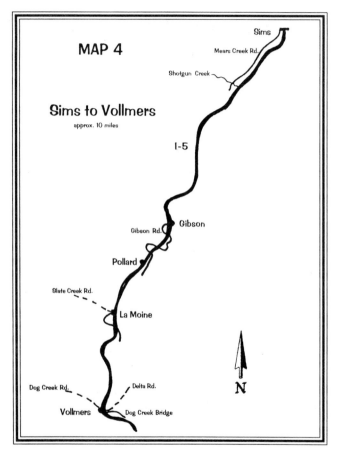

MAP 4

Sims to Vollmers

approx. 10 miles

Sims

Mears Creek Rd.

Shotgun Creek

I-5

Gibson

Gibson Rd.

Pollard

Slate Creek Rd.

La Moine

Dog Creek Rd.

Delta Rd.

Vollmers

Dog Creek Bridge

N

called Frontage Rd. This peaceful stretch of old highway leads us to Castle Crags State Park.

After a couple of miles, a left on Riverside Rd. takes us a short way off of our highway, across the river and to the pretty State Park picnic area that Highway 99 travelers doubtlessly picnicked in, and still do.

Back to Frontage Rd. and the deserted gas station/market at the intersection (p.115), then south to **Castella**, where the old highway is called Main St. after crossing Castle Creek on an old cement highway bridge. Here, on the north side of the creek, was the intersection of Highway 99 and Castle Creek Rd., the entrance to the main portion of the State Park, and the location of Ammiratti's Highway Grocery that served the campers and hikers. All of this was taken out by the freeway.

The old highway can be followed a short distance farther to the edge of Castella proper. Then our route disappears again and we must go back to Castle Creek Rd. and onto the southbound freeway near the modern rebuilt Ammiratti's near the new State Park entrance. (p.117)

Sweetbriar is the next exit. Through here was one of the major slide areas (See Chapter 11) in the canyon. From the east side of the freeway, we get a good look at the large slide to the south, now largely covered with young trees, and the realigned train tracks by taking the dirt road down to the right just after crossing the freeway overpass.(p.119)

Following Sweetbriar Rd. north, we're back on the old highway. It soon ends, having been blocked off near where the road turns a sharp right and turns into Falls Avenue. Return to the freeway.

Backtracking north on the freeway (p.119) toward Castella before continuing south reveals a couple more sights. Exit at the Vista Point. Look through the chain link fence and you can see the old roadbed of Highway 99 down below. Follow (on foot) up to where the freeway intersects it and discover another of the characteristic masonry rock walls, this one rudely broken off where a small freeway bridge begins. (p.78) Follow along the edge of the freeway and, lo and behold, under the bridge appears a short, curved piece of retaining wall that looks almost like an Indian cliff dwelling.

After turning back south on the freeway, we find the old highway again at **Conant** Rd. Turning south, we wind around, back under the freeway, and to an abrupt end. Heading north, the old highway ends more quickly. Back on the freeway, bypass the Flume Creek exit which leads us nowhere.

Sims to Vollmers: Map 4

At the **Sims** exit, go west to Mears Creek Rd., which is the old highway. A pretty 1929 concrete highway bridge crosses Mears Creek a short distance north of this intersection; shortly thereafter the old highway disappears where a dirt road heads sharply to the left going uphill. Turning south, we can travel the old highway for a couple of miles.

The road narrows, and we are now on a stretch of the earliest (pre-99) State Highway, for we soon reach the 1915 bridge crossing Shotgun Creek (see Chapter 10). Then we must backtrack and return to the freeway.

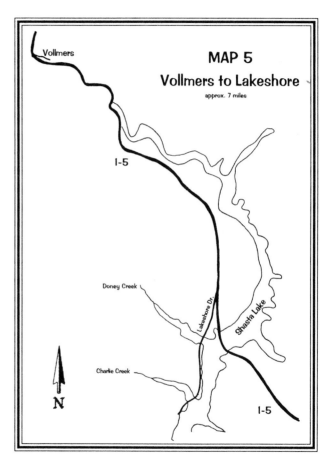

MAP 5
Vollmers to Lakeshore
approx. 7 miles

At the **Gibson** exit, turn right to reach one of the high points of our journey. On old Highway 99 again, we are led under the freeway and to a spot that so well illustrates the three basic phases of highway construction. In this one location, we cross a creek on a classic 1928 concrete bridge, while just upstream stands the original plain, narrow 1915 highway bridge. Above us stretch two sleek and massive freeway bridges (p. 121) The Sacramento River and the train tracks are only a few feet away.

Continuing, we wind past another nice stretch of rock retaining wall. Bypassing the Pollard Flat on ramp, the old highway is now called Eagle Roost Rd., and quickly ends. A large concrete arch bridge used to span **Pollard Gulch** but was torn down when the freeway came through, which we now must return to.

At the **LaMoine** Exit, turn right, and then left at the "school bus stop" sign. Here we encounter the 1927 bridge over Slate Creek (p. 123) with a very high rubble retaining wall providing a backdrop. After the crossing, the old highway climbs steeply and soon fizzles out.

The next exit, **Vollmers**, takes us to the acclaimed Harlan D. Miller bridge over Dog Creek. (p.125) To reach it, go to the east side of the freeway and take the road labeled "Not a Through Street." When the pavement ends, either drive or walk down the dirt road that takes you to the bridge. You will be well rewarded.

Vollmers to Lake Shore: Map 5

Our next 99 encounter will be at **Lakeshore** Dr., where we find a piece of the pre-Shasta Lake (see Chapter 12) highway. Turning south on Lakeshore Dr. (pp. 127, 128) we're on a short piece of pre-1943 highway that was not submerged by the lake. The main thrills are the two 1925 concrete arch bridges crossing Doney and Charlie Creeks whose decks have been raised to accommodate the lake waters. The amount of arch visible depends on the lake level. Lakeshore Dr. continues, but a short distance past Charlie Creek the old highway turned to the east into what is now lake. Backtrack to the freeway.

Salt Creek to Bridge Bay: Map 6

At the Gilman Rd./Salt Creek exit, turning north from the west side of the freeway takes us to Lower Salt Creek Rd., which encompasses a short piece of pre-lake highway way down by the lake. Then the old highway disappears into the **Salt Creek** inlet of Shasta Lake. During times of drought when the lake is low, vehicles drive out through the lake bed in search of water on makeshift roads. In this spot the makeshift road is a piece of pre-1942 Highway 99. Sections of pavement remain as well as a 1925 highway bridge usually well underwater (p. 129)—an exciting find!

It's the same situation at the **O'Brien**/Shasta Caverns exit, where the old highway to the north disappears into the O'Brien Creek inlet of the lake. As at Salt Creek, a concrete highway bridge (p.130) crossing O'Brien Creek made an appearance in 1994 when the lake was unusually low. On the other side of the freeway, the road down to Bailey Cove is another short stretch of pre-lake 99.

After crossing the long **Pit River** bridge (p. 133)

take the Bridge Bay exit down to the resort. Park and walk up the chained-off road heading back to the bridge and under it. This last part of the pre-lake highway we'll encounter leads up to the south approach of the original crossing of the Pit that is now submerged.

Mountain Gate to Red Bluff: Maps 7, 8A, 8

The old highway next emerges as we leave the canyon at the **Mountain Gate** exit, where it parallels the freeway both north and south of the exit for a short distance on Wonderland Blvd.

Back on the freeway, get off on the **Pine Grove** exit and turn south on Cascade Blvd. Soon on our right we pass one of the two "Giant Oranges" we will encounter, this one still in business. Soon after this the old highway reappears on the other side of the freeway, on Twin View Blvd., but we can't cross over until the Oasis Rd. overcrossing.

From Oasis Rd., turn south on Twin View (or you can go north for a short distance, but then you must return). Heading south, cross under the freeway and keep your eyes peeled for Valley Ridge Rd. on the left. Turn left and then immediately right on **North Boulder Dr.** which is an intact piece of 1920s highway. Look for a 1926 Kaiser Co. stamp in the concrete across from the KOA. Stay on this road up to East Lake Blvd. Turn right, then left on Market St. (called 273) which is the later Highway 99 going through Redding.

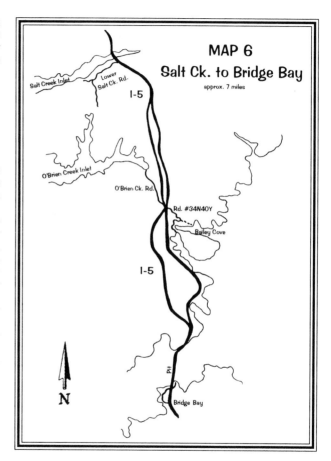

197

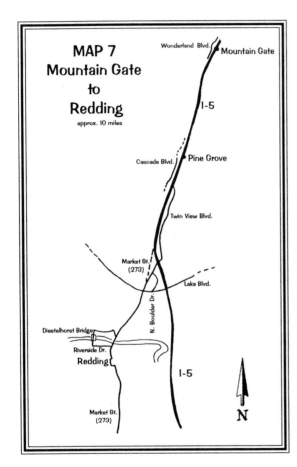

MAP 7
Mountain Gate
to
Redding
approx. 10 miles

Wonderland Blvd.
Mountain Gate

I-5

Cascade Blvd.
Pine Grove

Twin View Blvd.

Market St.
(273)

Lake Blvd.

N. Boulder Dr.

Diestelhorst Bridge
Riverside Dr.
Redding

I-5

Market St.
(273)

N

This piece of Highway 99 goes for almost fifteen miles, taking us through **Redding** and on to **Anderson**. The row of motels (p. 135) and businesses before Redding proper was called the "**Miracle Mile**." On the northwest corner of Mar Ave. just before the highway crosses the river is a nice example of a 1930s auto court once known as the Hidalgo Courts.(p.37)

Market St. crosses the river on a bridge built in 1936. Before that the highway looped over to the west and across the Diestelhorst Bridge (p.137) a couple of blocks upstream. To reach it take Riverside Dr. off of Market.

Market St. leads to downtown **Redding,** where at the intersection of Market and Yuba (p.140) a huge Christmas tree was placed in a manhole in the middle of the road during the holidays. This intersection is now encompassed by the downtown mall which ate a chunk out of Market. Nowadays you must travel on California St. (if going south) or Pine St. (if going north) for a few blocks.

Returning to Market St., or 273, it then follows the tracks down to **Anderson**, characterized in a 1930s guidebook as "dingy." Most of the original 1920s two lane Highway 99 lies under the northbound lanes of 273, which was the late 1940s U.S. 99 realignment.

A few short pieces of the 20s alignment remain near Anderson on the pre-1949 highway now called Barney St. The first piece is wedged between I-5 and 273 and accessed by turning east off of 273 onto Bruce St, then turning either left or right onto Barney. Going north, the road is now blocked at the nice old highway bridge over Anderson Creek; going south the old highway portion ends at the I-5 railroad overpass, but the road curves around and puts you back on 273.

To find the next disconnected piece of pre-1948 highway, from 273 turn east on Deschutes Rd. going past the Factory Stores. Right after going under the freeway, take a right on Locust St. until you reach the old highway, here called Barney Rd. It is shortly cut off by the freeway heading either north or south. The southern piece is single slab concrete with a hint of a center line.

Pick up the 99 trail again by returning to 273 and turning west on Rhonda Rd. You will soon be on a stretch of oak-lined old highway heading south, going up and around Cottonwood Hill. We spotted a "C Block" (see p. 182) through here. The old 99 highway ends at the south end of the small white-railed highway bridge. Stay on Rhonda to Gaspoint Rd. and turn east over the freeway.

99 reappears in the town of **Cottonwood** as Main St. The same 1930s guide book describes Cottonwood as "a scattered village of rutted winding streets, frame shanties, and red brick and frame false-front stores with wooden awnings." The town, like dozens of other small towns along Highway 99 during the thirties, was a bit run down, depressed and dependent on highway travelers for income. This piece of old highway ends after traveling south through town and crossing the impressive long bridge over Cottonwood Creek(p.145) and returning to I-5.

For the next few miles we cross rolling oak and grass country reminiscent of "old California". (p. 128) The concrete ribbon appears sporadically at several places along the base of the hills just west of the freeway, but most of it is gated. Notice it behind the truck scales near Bowman Rd. and at the Snively Rd. exit.

The next find is the humble little 1915 highway bridge lying between the north and southbound lanes of the freeway 7.5 miles south of Cottonwood, between Hooker Ck. Rd. and Jelly's Ferry exits.(p.129) For a closer look, it is more easily accessed from the northbound side of the freeway. This bridge was replaced in 1940 with the bridge that now carries northbound I-5.

A last short piece of old concrete highway before Red Bluff can be found by exiting at Wilcox Golf Rd. and turning right. The old highway starts at the golf course and again is soon blocked by a gate.

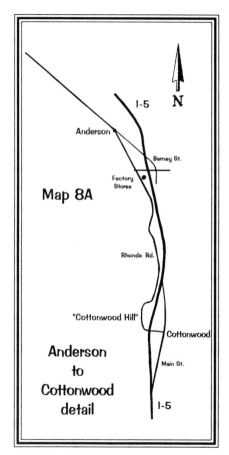

Map 8A

Anderson to Cottonwood detail

199

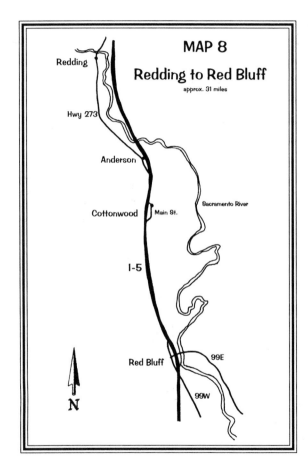

MAP 8

Redding to Red Bluff

approx. 31 miles

Redding

Hwy 273

Anderson

Cottonwood

Main St.

Sacramento River

I-5

Red Bluff

99E

99W

N

We pick up the trail again at the north **Red Bluff** exit. The white-railed bridge carrying traffic into town was the 1940 Highway 99 bridge. The earlier 1920s concrete road is quite visible in front of the wrecking yard near this bridge. It can be driven about 1/2 mile back north where it is gated. The concrete road can also be seen following beside the tracks south toward downtown.

Returning to the main road and heading south through town, don't miss the nice 1920 highway bridge that is easily overlooked since Main St. (the 1940s highway) currently bypasses it. Turn right on Breckenridge St. just off of Main and you'll find it immediately. An abandoned auto court at this location was recently leveled.

Return to Main and continue through town. **Red Bluff** had the distinction of being the farthest point upriver that the Sacramento River could be navigated, a significant fact in the days when road travel was difficult or impossible.

Red Bluff is where 99E and 99W diverge paths on their way to Sacramento.

99E—Red Bluff to Sacramento: Maps 9, 10, 11

This must have been the less favored route to the capital, for in the twenties the East Side Highway Association put up a series of billboards starting near the Oregon border urging travelers to "Turn Left at Red Bluff," directing their way with a giant left-pointing arrow painted on a Red Bluff building. 99E is the only part of the highway in northern California still actually designated as "State Highway 99."

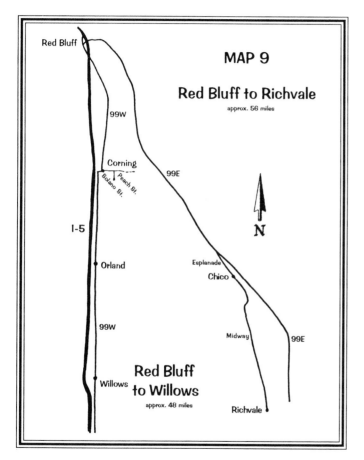

MAP 9

Red Bluff to Richvale

approx. 56 miles

Red Bluff

99W

Corning

Peach St.

Solano St.

99E

I-5

N

Orland

Esplanade

Chico

99W

Midway

99E

Red Bluff to Willows

approx. 48 miles

Willows

Richvale

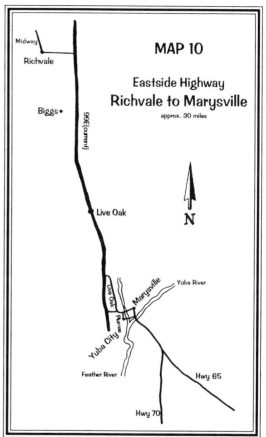

MAP 10

Eastside Highway
Richvale to Marysville

approx. 30 miles

Midway

Richvale

Biggs

99E (current)

N

Live Oak

Live Oak

Marysville

Yuba River

Plumas

Yuba City

Feather River

Hwy 65

Hwy 70

MAP 11

Eastside Highway
**Marysville to
Sacramento**

approx. 50 miles

Marysville

N. Beale Rd.

Rancho Rd.

Wheatland

Sheridan

99E
(current)

Hwy 70

Hwy 65

Lincoln

Industrial Ave.

Washington

Roseville

I-80

Auburn Blvd.

El Camino

W. Capital Blvd.

16th

Sacramento

N

In downtown **Red Bluff**, turn at the sign for Highways 36 and 99E (Antelope Blvd.), cross the river, take a left on Sale Lane and a right on Belle Mille Rd. On this short piece of old highway we cross two long concrete bridges with solid walls and then return to Antelope Blvd. A couple of miles later 99E splits from 36 and goes south.

It's a pastoral scene down this highway, as is 99W, but the crops are a little different on this side. Shady, park-like walnut groves dominate north of Chico. Prunes are another big crop. The little farm communities follow one after another, each having their little distinctions; **Dairyville**, **Los Molinos**, **Vina**, and larger, more sophisticated Chico.(pp. 146,147)

North of **Chico** today's 99 turns into freeway and follows a course to the east of the old route, so take the Business 99 turnoff. This takes us down Esplanade Blvd., former US 99.

As we reach downtown this splits into Main (northbound) and Broadway (southbound.) Stay on Business 99 until it turns at E Park Ave. and continue south on Midway Rd. We jog our way through the next string of small towns each of which once had the requisite motels and cafes to serve the traveling public; **Durham, Nelson, Richvale, Biggs, Gridley, Live Oak.** On 99 in Live Oak look for the Bicentennial Witness Tree, an over 200 year old valley oak, one of 35 trees nationwide so identified. At **Richvale** turn east on Richvale Hwy. to rejoin current 99 and turn south.

The old route next takes off on Live Oak Blvd, while what is now signed as 99E heads straight for the capital. The original route heads for the twin cities of **Yuba City** and **Marysville** (p.153), once known as "The Peach Bowl of America." Until 1946 the two towns were connected by the nineteen foot wide highway bridge over the Feather River built in 1906, now called the Twin Cities Memorial Bridge. A new bridge was built a few blocks north and the highway rerouted.

Live Oak Blvd. will merge onto Colusa Ave. Turn south on Plumas then east on Bridge St. to cross the older bridge. Across the Yuba River, through a railroad subway at the entrance to Marysville and on to 5th St. South on E St. to cross the Yuba River. Notice how Marysville is built below river level behind levees.

E St. merges onto Highway 70, but in less than a mile turn east onto N. Beale Rd., another piece of old 99. This road (called Lindhurst on the south end) goes along the tracks again for about three miles, then we're back on 70. Soon Highway 65 branches off of 70; take 65.

Back off at McGowan Parkway exit. East over to Rancho Rd., a tree-lined piece of former 99 we can follow for another few miles.(p.155) Near where Rancho Rd ends and we are forced back onto 65 at a place called Morrison's Crossing, is where the first groundbreaking on a state highway contract took place in the summer of 1912.

Back onto 65, the old route takes us through **Wheatland**, a small town beside the tracks, and on to **Lincoln**. Lincoln is still known for its terra cotta works; notice the huge stacks of red clay pipes at the plant on the edge of town.(p.157)

Right after Lincoln, veer off of 65 and onto Industrial, which again follows the tracks and has that "old highway" appearance. Industrial will eventually merge onto Washington for the last two miles into **Roseville**. Lincoln Rd. leaves Washington and will take you into the nicely preserved historic district. Lincoln was the earliest highway route, but to cross the tracks nowadays you must return to Washington St. and take the subway under the multiple tracks. Roseville is better known for its rail yards than its highway associations, although here is where 99 split from 40 after their joining in Davis.

After emerging from the subway, go up a block to Vernon St. and go west through downtown **Roseville** with its Tower Theater (p. 159) and other small town features. Turn south on Riverside.

Riverside turns into Auburn Blvd. and makes a sharp jog to the west after crossing I-80. Follow Auburn Blvd. all the way to El Camino and turn west, then south on Del Paso.(pp.160,161) You can follow Del Paso all the way to its end but must backtrack a block to get on the bridge to cross the American River. This bridge was built in 1941. Before that the crossing was inundated with high water on the average of eight days every winter.

After crossing the river, the road now splits into 12th St. southbound and 16th St. northbound. 16th was the 99E routing, although the exact alignments within **Sacramento** changed many times over the years.

99E and 99W met on Broadway.

99W—Red Bluff to Sacramento: Maps 9, 10,12

99W is well marked and easy to follow. Continue through **Red Bluff**, go under the freeway and we're on

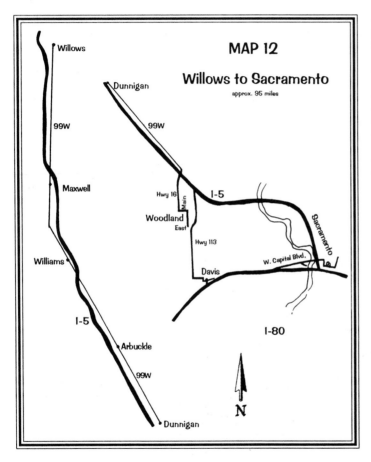

MAP 12

Willows to Sacramento

approx. 95 miles

Willows

Dunnigan

99W

99W

Maxwell

Hwy 16

I-5

Main

Woodland

East

Hwy 113

Williams

W. Capital Blvd.

Sacramento

Davis

I-5

I-80

Arbuckle

99W

Dunnigan

N

our way to another string of small agricultural/ former highway towns. Thus we visit **Proberta, Richfield** and **Corning.** (pp.163,165,167)) Most of the tall palms of which Corning was so proud froze out in 1972.

At **Corning**, 99 jogged to the right, going through town on Solano Ave. To find the site of the state's first municipal auto camp, instead turn east on Solano, then right on Peach St. to Woodson Park—this is it.

Return back west on Solano through town, then make another sharp left. The two treacherous right angle turns were well known to highway travelers. The second curve was the site of the Crook's Brothers service station (See illustration in Chapter 6). From here, it's a straight shot to **Orland.**(p.170)

The stretch from Corning to Orland had numerous road side attractions; glassblowers, a "snake pit," fruit stands, auto camps. We pass assorted remains of these places.

Orland welcomes us with a classic concrete arch built in 1926.(p.174) The one planned for the south end of town was never built.

As we continue our straight course south we enter the rice belt, with rice fields and grain elevators (p. 151) on either side of the road. After **Artois** (p.176) we enter a shady eucalyptus forest (p.177) near **Blue Gum** Rd. The motels here (p. 180) must have been favorites among 99 travelers and still appear to be nice places to stay. Check out the 1936 concrete bridge with solid sides and the patch of original concrete pavement that cuts across the current road ½ mile south of the Grove Motel.

Still on a well-marked 99W, next it's **Willows** (p. 111)**, Maxwell, Williams, Arbuckle, Dunnigan, Zamora.** The ten miles north and south of Williams were known as Blood Alley because of the number of gruesome accidents that used to occur along this straight speed-inspiring stretch of road. ◄

Williams also has an arch (p.175) but it doesn't span the old highway. Built in 1917, it spanned E St. so it could be easily seen by railroad passengers. Just south of Willows an abandoned Giant Orange sits beside the road.(p.179)

Soon after **Zamora** (p.183) 99W crosses Cache Creek on a 1930s concrete arch bridge, right next to the metal truss railroad bridge.(p.185) To see it at all you must park and walk for a look underneath.

99W soon ends. Cross over I-5 to reconnect to the old route to **Woodland** on Highway 16. Turn east on Main through the still vigorous downtown, cross the tracks and turn south on East St.(p.186) But before continuing you might want to marvel at some beautifully restored trucks the likes of which once plied old 99 at the Hayes Antique Truck Museum (1962 Hayes Lane, Woodland.)

East St., the former 99 route to **Davis**, has been replaced by Highway 113. But you can follow walnut-lined East St. along the tracks for about 2½ mi. It ends where the old road used to cross the tracks. Another short stretch is visible across the tracks; this is accessed off of 113 at Road 27.

Backtrack to Road 25A to get on 113. Off at Davis on Russell Blvd., east to B St., south to 1ˢᵗ St.,

east three blocks to Richards Blvd. After going under the 1916 subway that separated the highway from the tracks, turn east on Olive Dr. This half mile stretch has the old highway "feel", complete with old auto/trailer court and gas station (now housing a barber shop.) Return to Richards and get on I-80 heading east.

Davis is where US 99 once united with US 40 for the final few miles to the capital. I-80 now covers most of that distance. We cross the **Yolo Causeway** (p.82) on the freeway and pick up the old trail again at West Capital Blvd., with its row of motels that have definitely seen better days. At the approach to the river off of West Capital on Tower Court is a 300' long piece of old concrete highway locked behind a chainlink fence, a remnant from the 1911 approach to the M St. Bridge.

That bridge was replaced by the imposing **Tower Bridge** (p.188) in 1936. A walk across it is worth the effort.

And so old Route 99 carries us across the Sacramento River for one last time on the only pre-WWII vertical lift bridge in California, and to the capitol building straight ahead. South on 5ᵗʰ St. to Broadway, where 99W and 99E joined to continue on south all the way to the Mexican border.

We've reached our destination!

Allen, Marion V. *Redding and the Three Shastas*. Self-published, 1989.

Baeder, John. *Gas, Food, and Lodging*. Abbeville Press, New York, 1982.

Ballanger, Craig. *Shasta's Headwaters*. Frank Amato Publications, Inc. Portland, OR, 1998.

Belasco, Warren James. *Americans on the Road: From Autocamp to Motel, 1910-1945*. MIT Press, Cambridge, MA, 1979.

Bird, Jackson. "The History of a State Highway Across Central California; 1895-1919," M.A. dissertation, U.C. Berkeley, 1950.

"The Bridge Story." *Weed Press*, 5/31/1978.

Buckley, Patricia R. *Highway 99: A California Chronicle*. Self-published, 1987.

Buckley, Patricia R. *Those Unforgettable Giant Oranges*. Self-published, 1987

Boudier, William. *The Paths of Humanity*. CA Division of Highways, 1966.

Built in the U.S.A. National Trust for Historic Preservation, Preservation Press, Washington D.C., 1985.

California Highways and Public Works. California Department of Transportation, various issues.

The California Motorist. California State Automobile Association, 1918.

Check the Oil Magazine. January 1995, March 1995, May 1995, August 1999.

The Covered Wagon. Shasta Historical Society, various volumes.

Dewey, Louie. "A Short History of Cave Springs." *Dunsmuir Centennial*, 1985.

Donley, Michael, et al. *Atlas of California*. Pacific Book Center, Culver City, CA,1979.

Drury, Aubrey. *California, An Intimate Guide*. Harper and Bros., 1939.

Encyclopedia Britannica. Volume 15, Page 896. Chicago, 1976.

Evarts, John, editor. *Oaks of California.*. Cachuma Press, Inc., Los Olivos, CA, 1992.

Fireman's Fund of California. *Automobile Tour Book of California*,1918.

Hamilton, E. E. *Thorpe's Illustrated Road Map and Tour Book of California*, 1911.

Hanson, Harry, editor. *California, A Guide to the Golden State*. American Guide Series. Federal Writer's Project, Hastings House, NY, 1939.

Historic Highway Bridges of California. California Department of Transportation, 1990.

Hopfinger, Tony. "New Dam Lets Town Stay Put." *Redding Record Searchlight,* June 10, 1999.

International Pacific Highways System.. Automobile Club of Southern California, Los Angeles, CA,1934.

Jakle, John A. and Keith A. Sculle. *The Gas Station in America*. Johns Hopkins University Press, Baltimore, 1994.

Johnson, Stephen, Robert Dawson, and Gerald Haslam. *The Great Central Valley, California's Heartland*. UC Press, 1993.

Leibs, Chester H. *Main Street to Miracle Mile*. Johns Hopkins University Press, Baltimore, 1995.

Lewis, Tom. *Divided Highways*. Viking, 1997.

McGowan, Joseph A., PhD. *History of the Sacramento Valley*. Lewis Historical Publishing Company, New York, 1961.

Motor Guide to California.. National Automobile Club, San Francisco, 1926.

Motorland. California State Automobile Association, June 1922 and August 1931.

National Motorist. National Automobile Club, Feb. 1932.

Reid, Dixie. "On the Road," *Sacramento Bee,* 12/10/1987.

Rider, Fremont. *Rider's California.* 1928.

Roggero, Alex with Tony Beadle. *Go Greyhound.* Barnes and Noble Books, New York, 1996.

Rolle, Andrew F. *California, A History.* Thomas Y. Crowell Company, New York, 1963.

Root, Norman. "A Century of Good Roads," unpublished paper, CalTrans Centennial Coordinating Committee, Nov. 17, 1994.

The Siskiyou Pioneer. Siskiyou County Historical Society, various volumes.

Weir, Kim. *Northern California Handbook.* Moon Publications, Chico, CA, 1990.

Winn, Bernard C. *Arch Rivals: 90 Years of Welcome Arches in Small-Town America.* Incline Press, Enumclaw, WA 1993.

Interviews and correspondence with:

    Sisson Museum, Mt. Shasta
    Redding Museum of Art and History (now called Turtle Bay Museum)
    Corning Museum
    CalTrans Library
    Mike Ballard, Patrick Frank, Robert Pomeroy, Doug Pruitt, Charles Smith, Joel Windmiller (including his web site)

Table of contents for
That Ribbon of Highway II: Highway 99 from the State Capital to the Mexican Border

PART 1

Table of contents for
That Ribbon of Highway III:
Highway 99 through the Pacific Northwest

Own **ALL THREE** books!

LIVING GOLD PRESS

P.O. Box 2
Klamath River, CA 96050
www.LivingGoldPress.com
jandk@livinggoldpress.com